Rethink

Rethink

Leading Voices on Life After Crisis and
How We Can Make a Better World

EDITED BY
AMOL RAJAN

Licensed by the BBC

© BBC 2021

BBC Books, an imprint of Ebury Publishing
20 Vauxhall Bridge Road, London SW1V 2SA

BBC Books is part of the Penguin Random House group of companies
whose addresses can be found at global.penguinrandomhouse.com

Penguin
Random House
UK

Amol Rajan has asserted his right to be identified as the author
of the introductions of this Work in accordance with the
Copyright, Designs and Patents Act 1988

Introductions © 2021 Amol Rajan
Rethink is licensed by the BBC © BBC 2021

First published by BBC Books in 2021
Paperback edition published in 2022

www.penguin.co.uk

A CIP catalogue record for this book is available from the British Library

ISBN 9781785947186

Editorial Director: Albert DePetrillo
Assistant Editor: Daniel Sørensen
Project Editors: Grace Paul and Steve Tribe
Design and typesetting: seagulls.net

Printed and bound in Great Britain by Clays Ltd, Elcograf S.p.A.

The authorised representative in the EEA is Penguin Random House Ireland,
Morrison Chambers, 32 Nassau Street, Dublin D02 YH68

Penguin Random House is committed to a sustainable future for
our business, our readers and our planet. This book is made
from Forest Stewardship Council® certified paper.

CONTENTS

AMOL RAJAN *Introduction* 1

WHO WE ARE

CARLO ROVELLI *Rethinking Humanity* 29

POPE FRANCIS *Rethinking Poverty* 32

PETER HENNESSY *Rethinking Democracy* 36

ANAND GIRIDHARADAS *Rethinking Capitalism* 40

JARED DIAMOND *Rethinking a Global Response* 44

ZIAUDDIN SARDAR *Rethinking Normality* 48

DALAI LAMA *Rethinking Ancient Wisdom* 52

C.K. LAL *Rethinking Institutions* 55

JARVIS COCKER *Rethinking an Environmental Revolution* 59

CLARE CHAMBERS *Rethinking the Body* 63

STEVEN PINKER *Rethinking Human Nature* 67

TOM RIVETT-CARNAC *Rethinking History* 71

JONATHAN SUMPTION *Rethinking the State* 75

WHAT WE DO

DAVID SKELTON *Rethinking Industry* 81

EMMA GRIFFIN *Rethinking Work* 85

CALEB FEMI *Rethinking Education* 88

GINA MCCARTHY *Rethinking Activism* 92

TARA WESTOVER *Rethinking the Education Divide* 95

KWAME ANTHONY APPIAH *Rethinking the Power of Small Actions* 100

CHARLOTTE LYDIA RILEY *Rethinking Universities* 104

K.K. SHAILAJA *Rethinking Development* 108

SAMANTHA POWER *Rethinking Global Governance* 111

KT TUNSTALL *Rethinking the Music Industry* 115

REBECCA ADLINGTON *Rethinking the Athlete's Life* 119

BRENDA HALE *Rethinking How We Do Trials* 124

NISHA KATONA *Rethinking Hospitality* 128

KATHERINE GRAINGER *Rethinking the Olympics* 132

DAVID GRAEBER *Rethinking Jobs* 136

JAMES HARDING *Rethinking News* 140

CAROLYN MCCALL *Rethinking Television* 146

HOW WE FEEL

MOHAMMED HANIF *Rethinking Intimacy* 155

H.R. MCMASTER *Rethinking Empathy* 159

CAROL COOPER *Rethinking Racial Equality* 162

PAUL KRUGMAN *Rethinking Solidarity* 166

AMONGE SINXOTO *Rethinking Safety* 169

REED HASTINGS *Rethinking Togetherness* 173

KANG KYUNG-WHA *Rethinking Accountability* 177

LUCY JONES *Rethinking Biophilia* 180

COLIN JACKSON *Rethinking Our Responsibility for Our Health* 184

MIRABELLE MORAH *Rethinking Ourselves* 188

NICCI GERRARD *Rethinking Old Age* 192

BRIAN ENO *Rethinking the Winners* 196

JUDE BROWNE *Rethinking Responsibility* 200

ELIF SHAFAK *Rethinking Uncertainty* 205

HOW WE LIVE

AMANDA LEVETE *Rethinking How We Live* 213

NIALL FERGUSON *Rethinking Progress* 217

DAVID WALLACE-WELLS *Rethinking Consensus* 223

MARGARET MACMILLAN *Rethinking International Cooperation* 227

HRH THE PRINCE OF WALES *Rethinking Nature* 231

ONORA O'NEILL *Rethinking Digital Power* 236

MATTHEW WALKER *Rethinking Sleep* 239

HENRY DIMBLEBY *Rethinking How We Eat* 243

ELIZA MANNINGHAM-BULLER *Rethinking Health Inequality* 247

XINE YAO *Rethinking Masks* 251

GEORGE SOROS *Rethinking Debt* 255

MARIANA MAZZUCATO *Rethinking Value* 258

DOUGLAS ALEXANDER *Rethinking Economic Dignity* 264

EVAN SPIEGEL *Rethinking Long-Term Success* 268

WHERE WE GO

PETER FRANKOPAN *Rethinking Asia* 275

STUART RUSSELL *Rethinking AI* 279

V.S. RAMACHANDRAN *Rethinking Brains* 283

SEB EMINA *Rethinking Travel* 288

AARON BASTANI *Rethinking an Ageing Population* 292

RANA FOROOHAR *Rethinking Data* 299

ANTHONY TOWNSEND *Rethinking Robots* 303

AMOL RAJAN *Postscript* 309

Contributors 315

Credits 343

INTRODUCTION

Plague, revolution, war and famine are the customary means by which particular years mark the beginning and end of epochs. In modern history, 1666, 1776, 1848, 1918 and 1945 all have outsize influence on our imaginations. They mark not just the end of an era, but of some vaster chapter in the story of our species, defined by distinctive forces, ideas and events. The year 2020 always had a landmark ring to it. Now, because of Covid-19, a respiratory virus named after the year it emerged, future historians will also write about a world BC and AD: Before Coronavirus and After the Disease. What happens next, to adapt a ubiquitous quote by the economist Milton Friedman, depends not just on the power of the ideas lying around, but the ideas of those around us with most power, whether individual or institutional.

Friedman's observation obeyed an iron law of famous political quotations: namely, the much more interesting sentence that followed is largely forgotten. He went on to say, referring to the intellects of his day: 'That, I believe, is our basic function: to develop alternatives to existing policies; to keep them alive and available until the politically impossible becomes the politically inevitable.'

This is the starting point for *Rethink* – and an invitation to you.

For several years now, and long before most of us had heard the word 'coronavirus', I have argued that we are living through one of history's epoch shifts. Three giant forces – ecological devastation, a technological revolution and Easternisation – mean that we entered 2020 having already experienced years of dizzying, and dislocating, change. In short order, we have seen the worst financial crash since 1929, the Arab Spring and a global surge in authoritarian populism. Now, the first pandemic in a century is brutal confirmation of just how momentous this period in our lives is. It is a catalyst for many of the deep global trends already underway. And also a prompt for new habits, innovations and cultural change.

It is often said, including by some of our essayists in the pages that follow, that pandemics don't create new trends so much as accelerate underlying ones. In fact, they do both. Covid-19 has done *a lot* of both. The result is we are living through history's greatest acceleration – one which, alas, is leaving much of humanity behind. Several dichotomies have emerged in recent years to explain the realignments of politics around the world: open vs closed; Anywhere vs Somewhere; democratic vs authoritarian. Perhaps the most useful of all is one that policymakers have largely neglected: fast vs slow. In a world that is not just speeding up, but doing so at an accelerating rate, countless people are being left behind, their voices often unheard and their interests often neglected.

For most of the twentieth century, politics in the West was divided along a socio-economic axis – that is, class. Political institutions, from parties to parliament, reflected this. Today, politics is divided along a socio-cultural axis. In the 2019 election, the two main British parties in effect flipped: the Tories are no longer the party of the rich, and Labour no more the party of the poor. Of course there is crossover, but the party bases have inverted. Cultural values, and in particular attitude to change, drives allegiance, and one of the biggest influences on it is the extent of your education.

Mass immigration is often cited as the key change in post-war Britain. Mass education gets less attention. But its effects are enormous, and only now being truly felt. The rapid expansion of the university sector has created a massive divide – degrees of separation, you might call it – which strongly predicts voting intention. With Brexit, as with the election of Donald Trump, the second-best indicator of how people would vote, after skin colour, was whether or not they had a degree. Those without degrees were much, much more likely to vote for Brexit or Trump. No wonder he declared, during his campaign, 'I love the poorly educated!'

This is not because people who voted for Brexit or Trump are stupid. It is more because in a world of dizzying, even frightening change, a degree and all that comes with it can give you the confidence, capital and connections to thrive amid a world in flux. For the mobile and highly educated, change – sometimes called disruption – can mean gain. For the less well educated, who live close to where they grew up, or in neglected towns, change means pain. Disruption isn't something cool to be embraced. Disruption is a lost way of life.

Fast vs slow, then, is the governing paradigm of our times. And the internet, and associated explosion in media, means the times come at us faster than ever. This is the too-much-information age. It's hard and getting harder to keep up with seismic events.

Yet one common experience of this pandemic is that it has allowed us to slow down, even stop, and try to make sense of all this disruption. Lockdown gives you perspective. If some good is to come of all this suffering, now is the moment to take stock, to ask not just what is happening, but why we are going so badly wrong, in so many ways, all at the same time. And to plot how we might do things differently.

The essayists for *Rethink* have done just that. In this introduction, I want to outline the intellectual climate and historic moment into which their clever, and often radical, contributions have been flung; and to draw out some of the threads and themes common to all. And I want to be upfront about the mixed emotions of these essays, captured in the very word 'Rethink'. There is a gap between the essential optimism of the project, and the grimness not just of Covid-19, but of many of the threats we face.

If you are reading this in the affluent West, it is completely reasonable to feel that the Burkean contract between the generations, in which life gets better for our children, is shattered; that inequality is worsening; that across the globe power is being consolidated among ever fewer people; that climate change is an existential threat to our species currently lacking an adequate response; and that the great promise of the digital revolution has given way to a new oligarchy, a degradation of the truth and the disintegration of our public domain.

To recognise all this is realism, not pessimism. To rethink it is to inject hope where doom would otherwise prevail, and to spur action that can deliver sanctuary, or even salvation, from the gathering storm.

Those three giant forces – ecological devastation, technological revolution and Easternisation – were deeply entrenched before the malfeasance of that hungry bat in Wuhan, if indeed it is the culprit, unleashed such ruin. Let's take them in reverse order.

Covid-19 marks the end of the American century. The post-1945 world order was a geopolitical settlement with the following features: American leadership of a rules-based system, upheld by key global institutions, converging towards political liberalism and open markets, if not outright democracy.

Today, every single element of that world is either under pressure or going into reverse. Under President Trump, America retreated from the world it had created. This will itself be reversed by President Biden, but huge damage to alliances has been done. The norms by which international laws are upheld have been flagrantly violated by assertive rivals to American hegemony, especially autocratic Russia and China. Several global institutions, from Nato to the World Trade Organisation, are enduring a crisis of confidence and seeing rivals emerge. Illiberal democracy is gaining ground on liberal democracy, often from within. A squad of strongman leaders are competing with each other to be most fierce. Commitment to free trade – a shibboleth at the turn of the century – has collapsed, under the weight of some evidence, and a growing feeling, that globalisation has, at least in the affluent West, helped the rich but hurt the poor.

Above all, a radical shift in economic power to the East is being followed by a radical shift in political power to the East. For more than 500 years, the locus of global history has been in the conflicts between European empires, and then states, and then their progeny. As historian Peter Frankopan argues in his essay (see page 275), this is the Asian century. That locus will shift to the East, with conflicts – at least those involving physical armies – likely to erupt when the concentric circles of influence around competing Great Powers collide. Geopolitics will revive features of the late nineteenth century onwards, when friction between empires delivered ruin.

In 2018, I made a documentary for Radio 4 called *The Decline of the West*, marking the centenary of Oswald Spengler's dense but seminal work of the same name. Spengler had seen the devastation wrought on Germany by the Great War, and figured that twilight was settling on a great civilisation. He was wrong – or rather very premature – partly because in mid-century America, extraordinary leadership would mix with industrial glory to extend the dominance of western ideas and values. This time, the West is unlikely to be so lucky, and for one reason above all: demography.

The secret engine of global history is the youth bulge. If you want to look for where history is going to be made, look for a big surge and swell in the proportion of young people. Not because there is anything wrong with old people, of course. Young people are just fitter, able to work longer, don't cost a huge amount to look after, and have a greater appetite for the kind of risk-taking that can spur innovation and economic dynamism.

In 1945, the West was twice young. First, it was young in the sense that the very idea of the West – that rules-based order, led by America, enforced by western-led global institutions – was itself fresh. But the West was also young in a more literal sense: its people were young. There was a sharp rise in births in 1920, after the Great War and Spanish flu. And then there was another sharp rise in birth in the years after 1945. This created the Baby Boomer generation. The cultural energy and radicalism of the 1960s is attributed by some historians to the fact that a very large cohort entered adulthood at the same time. Relative to the rest of the population, the number of people in their early twenties swelled.

Today, the West is very old. The Baby Boomers, more likely to vote for Brexit or Donald Trump, and to die from Covid-19, mean that Europe and America are turning grey at an extraordinary rate. Aaron Bastani's essay (see page 292), one of many here that made me change my mind, helped me realise that confronting the social and economic consequences of an ageing population is our single most urgent policy challenge. I used to think it was climate change, but at least on that issue there is widespread awareness and an emerging consensus. How many public intellectuals or politicians have given deep thought to the fact that, as Bastani argues, for the first time in the history of our species, the old will outnumber the young?

This explosion in not just old people, but very old people, all of whom we love and want to care for, will coincide with the first reduction of the working-age population – and its tax base – in our history (see Nicci Gerrard's essay, page 192). The consequences will be profound. Imagine an entire world turning Japanese: a country whose remarkable growth a few decades ago has given way to stagnation, partly because of demography.

And here's the rub: it is western countries that are ageing fastest. This is partly because we have recently talked so much about death we've overlooked births. British fertility is collapsing. The replacement rate – the number of children that would need to be born per woman to keep the population stable, is 2.1. In 2012, in England and Wales, it was 1.9. Now it is 1.6: the lowest figure since comparable records began in 1938. The scandal of housing policy – a cynical state failure compounding a monumental market failure – means young couples just don't get a home until much later in life, if at all. In 1980, the average British woman got married at around 23, and man at around 25. In 2017, it was 35 and 38. We have invented an entirely new chapter in our lives: the odyssey years. Fewer babies will be born. Many more IVF doctors will become very rich. And little noticed, and even less lamented, the western nuclear family will continue its steady disintegration, replaced by a hodgepodge of kinship arrangements.

That housing scandal is in fact an assortment of smaller scandals, from the handing of contracts to favoured developers and political donors, to the desecration of urban landscapes through grim, imprisoning architecture built with utility rather than civility or beauty in mind. Another is the failure to build more houses, partly because of a peculiarly pastoral and British mythology around something called the Green Belt, the reality of which bears no relation to the phrase in common parlance. It isn't green, it isn't a belt, and there isn't just one of them. In fact, there are 14, often mostly brown. Misunderstood as conservation zones, planning rules in these areas have barely been touched since their introduction in 1955, and prevent sensible development in precisely the areas around our big cities that will be most in demand after the pandemic, as I explain below.

Today, the youth bulge – where history is made – is elsewhere: in places like Nigeria and India, the latter adding a million workers – many of them highly educated; almost all of them energetic and enterprising; many of them, I must admit, related to me – to the labour market every single month. The baby boom of Lagos and New Delhi will coincide with a demographic crunch in London and New York. China has noticed, and is worried: so much so that in 2013 it abandoned its one-child policy.

In 2020, Asia's GDP overtook the rest of the world combined. It will rise to 60 per cent by 2030. The US economy probably won't return to its pre-pandemic size until 2022. By then, China's will have grown 10 per cent. The Centre for Economics and Business Research (CEBR) has predicted that, because of Covid-19, China will overtake the US as the world's largest economy in dollar terms by 2028 – five years sooner than previously predicted. Two years later, India's economy will be the third biggest in the world. This is an excellent example of the speeding up of history *itself* speeding up.

In the nineteenth century, imperial Britain ruled the world. In the twentieth century, the democratic United States was in charge. In this century, as the journalist Andrew Neil has written, a Communist-capitalist geron-tocracy home to the world's oldest known civilisation is aggressively pursuing the status of top dog. Is that what you want? Are you ready?

All this amounts to Easternisation – not globalisa-tion, as it is sometimes lazily called. Globalisation was an earlier period, and process, in which goods, capital and ideas became part of global supply chains. Easternisation is about the rise of Asia and the decline of the West.

To the extent that these two processes are related, the quality of government is a determining factor. This is not a fashionable issue, except in the sense that it is a common refrain for the pub bore who wants to whinge that 'it's all the government's fault'. The thing is, with Covid-19, that complaint might have been valid. The pandemic has made very clear that improving the calibre and competence of institutional leaders everywhere, and particularly in governments, is critical.

(Can it be mere coincidence, by the way, that so many of the countries thought to have handled the pandemic well – Germany, New Zealand, Taiwan – are led by women?)

Half a millennium ago, when China's empire was a world power, it had the best government, selecting 'Mandarin' civil servants by exacting written examinations. For centuries, it continued to focus on teaching classical Confucianism rather than modern science, whereas European powers made the most of the Enlightenment, investing in science and technology. Today, Chinese leadership has a laser-like focus on cutting-edge technologies, and the Communist Party scours the country recruiting exceptional talent to its cause. Indeed, not only has China embraced big government, but it has been followed by several other Asian countries – among them Thailand, Malaysia, Japan – whose lavish spending, high-tech surveillance and relaxation about debt has suddenly overturned decades of preference for a smaller state.

Two of the countries most feted for their response to the pandemic, South Korea and Singapore, have one thing in common: their best minds go into government. Not politics, but civil service, where they are rewarded with social esteem and big salaries. It may not be high on the agenda, especially at a time of stretched finances, but if improving the calibre of government is urgent, it may be that civil servants, like teachers, need to be paid more.

That requires taxation to change: taxing different activities, or different people, different amounts.

All of which, by the way, is extremely hard to do. It remains one of the most deeply rooted superstitions of our age that all social and economic problems are capable of political solutions. They are not. Policy is hard, involves trade-offs, and has unforeseeable and unintended consequences, often far away. For instance, the failure to build more houses in the Chilterns, west of London, because of a misunderstanding of the 'Green Belt', has contributed to a housing crisis, which has contributed to a collapse in the number of babies being born in Britain, which has contributed to the demographic crunch facing the West. Thus are the destinies of the Chilterns and Chennai entwined. In an age of deeply embedded networks of goods, information, capital and labour, the sheer complexity of our systems of government connects us, however remotely, to people far away. And yet the incentives of different groups of voters within the same country rarely align – let alone those in different ones. A dose of realism about what effective government can and can't achieve is overdue. It's not fashionable to argue this, but governments that keep the peace and deliver rising wages are the exception and not the rule.

Ahead of civil servants in the queue for public affection are other 'key workers', particularly those in health and the caring professions. During the pandemic, weekly applause broke out in streets across Britain, an expression of gratitude and solidarity. You probably know people who work in health or care, and they've probably mentioned that while applause is nice, even lovely, higher wages would be lovelier.

No line from the *Rethink* project has resonated with me as much as one from David Graeber's essay (see page 136), written and recorded shortly before he died. 'The more obviously your work benefits other people, the less they pay you.' Think about that for a moment. The social or moral value of jobs today has become largely unmoored from their economic value – that is, the price of labour, or wage. At the time of writing, widespread revulsion at this fact has not led to any practical change. This is the subject of Mariana Mazzucato's essay (see page 258).

Not coincidentally, inequality of wealth and opportunity (which is different to inequality of income) was growing before the pandemic – and has been radically worsened by it. The Burkean emotional and moral contract between the generations, by which our children have a better quality of life than our parents, is broken, at least in the West. It's still realistic in much of Asia and sub-Saharan Africa, and part of the Middle East.

In Europe and America, ultra-low interest rates since the financial crash have led to massive inflation in asset prices: a huge transfer of wealth to the already rich. Many people in their twenties and thirties, even those on decent salaries, will never own a house. The generous pensions of the mid-1990s are extinct. University, once free, is now debt-laden. And the labour market that today's young people are entering has tipped the balance between security and flexibility towards the latter: zero-hours contracts and the gig economy have brought with them huge insecurity. It's past time, as Peter Hennessy argues (see page 36), for a modern Beveridge. The position is vacant, should you wish to apply.

If key workers are underpaid, and quality of life is falling, a consensus has emerged that our economic arrangements in the West are failing. That this should happen at the same time as our political arrangements are so convulsed, with polarisation and a yawning values divide (strongly correlated with education), suggests something deeper may need a rethink. And what connects the economics and politics of the West over the past generation is liberalism.

Liberalism is going out of fashion. Criticised from the left for its economic consequences (particularly growing inequality) and from the right for its political effects (an inflation in rights without a corresponding inflation in duties), this western idea is exhausted. That is not to say it is wrong; just that it is probably *insufficient* to answer the challenges of today.

Liberalism is a framework of rules and institutions. If society were our home, it would provide the bricks and mortar, and a bit of prior scaffolding, but be silent on the contents inside. That has been its traditional strength: staying quiet on how society should be provides space for everyone to offer their vision. In plural times, this is valuable. But in unequal and anxious times it feels like complacency. Liberalism's silence on the good life, its refusal to prescribe or proscribe how we should live, feels lazy when we are stumbling into a new epoch. Joe Biden, Angela Merkel, Emmanuel Macron and Justin Trudeau may all be relative moderates, but they are being buffeted by populism, and do not boast of their centrist credentials in the manner that, say, Tony Blair did a generation ago. We are all post-liberals now.

Even in Silicon Valley. It is one of the great ironies of our age that the class of super-rich technologists and engineers that has emerged in California has its intellectual and moral foundations in the counterculture of the 1960s. Big Tech is what happened when the flower-power generation sobered up.

Steve Jobs, its spiritual leader, was a Buddhist. His generation of visionaries were profoundly anti-materialistic at the start of their careers, and unfathomably rich at the end. Their worldview was, and is, anti-government. In Europe, and particularly Berlin and Brussels, there is a deep belief that social problems are capable of legal and regulatory solutions – that is, those wielded by a smart state. In California, the new data kings believe that social problems have technological solutions.

This has made them generally hostile to Washington, and to bureaucracies everywhere; but it is changing, as growing concern about the social harms, and economic power, of these companies leads to a new settlement between technology and democracy. It is also a point of difference between America and China. In the former, technology companies are separate from, and often hostile to, legislators. Mark Zuckerberg can suspend Donald Trump from his platform, and the latter is powerless to act. But in China, the biggest technology companies are extensions of the state: sponsored, and ultimately controlled, by the Chinese Communist Party. When Jack Ma, China's richest and perhaps most famous man, gave a speech criticising the party, he was soon forced into hiding, and billions were wiped off the value of Alibaba, the e-commerce giant he founded. In China, the web is a tool of surveillance, and reinforces authoritarian rule.

The contest between these visions of digital life will shape humanity's future. There is no such thing as 'the' internet today. There are competing digital domains, and a tech Cold War. With half of humanity yet to come online, the question of which domain they join – a libertarian, Californian one dominated by a few data kings, or a Chinese walled garden – is one of the most consequential questions of the age.

You may not have heard of the Chinese tech giants, but their scale is daunting. According to Goldman Sachs,

India's entire internet economy is worth $60 billion. On Singles Day, a 24-hour shopping extravaganza, Alibaba did sales of $74 billion.

For states that are not democratic, such as China, Saudi Arabia or Russia, digital technology affords a chance to control a population, project national power and create general wealth. For democracies, digital technology affords a chance to do the last of these – though most of the wealth goes to the companies themselves, who employ relatively few people – and make society more attractive to live in. This requires the risks to be managed. Over the past 15 years, they haven't been managed at all, and companies such as Facebook, Google and Apple have largely had free rein. That is changing. A new deal between technology and democracy is slowly emerging. In their essays, philosopher Onora O'Neill and journalist Rana Foroohar (see pages 236 and 299) explore what this new deal might look like.

Fundamental to it is a recognition of the power of data. I said earlier this is the Age of Asia. It is also the Age of Data. Apple is a hardware firm. But Facebook, Google, Amazon, Alibaba and, increasingly, Microsoft, are data firms. Their power comes from data: owning it and selling it. The data is largely about me and you. Facebook and Google, extensions of the twentieth-century advertising industry, sell that data to companies who want to target us. It is sometimes said by those concerned about the new data kings that data is the new oil: a reference to the monopolistic tendencies of American oil barons a century ago. This is naïve.

Data is not like oil. The whole point about oil is that it is finite; the whole point about data is that it is super-abundant. In this respect, it is more like sunlight. Data can be re-used. Oil cannot. And whereas oil is owned by the fortunate baron or king (rarely queen, alas) who owns the ground above it, the ownership of data is an open question. Capitalism, to acquire consent, must spread ownership. Spreading the ownership of data is one of the most complex but enticing policy questions we face today, and something our essayists grapple with.

It is a mark of the speed at which innovation happens that several of the companies I mention didn't exist two decades ago. At the time of writing, the richest man in the world is Elon Musk. He has that wealth because investors are piling into his electric car company, Tesla – another company that didn't exist before the turn of the century.

And though it is hard to comprehend, the rate at which technology is changing our lives is almost certain to speed up, not slow down, as our current digital revolution is succeeded by a series of digital revolutions – in artificial intelligence (see Stuart Russell, page 279) and quantum computing particularly. Some of it will be powered by graphene, the 'miracle material' discovered at the University of Manchester in 2004. Better at conducting electricity than copper; 200 times stronger than steel but six times lighter; and almost perfectly transparent, it could be that graphene powers the next industrial revolution.

That revolution will be green. It has to be. At the softer end of the international scientific consensus on anthropomorphic global heating, my children could well be under water by the time they reach old age.

Of the three giant forces reshaping our lives, ecological catastrophe occupies the most attention among our essayists, but will detain me least here. The reason for that is we all know what needs to be done and the essayists put it much better than I ever could. Prince Charles, an environmentalist for more than half a century, makes the case for a relationship between Sapiens and this blue marble we call home based on harmony (page 231). Jarvis Cocker's essay (page 59) concurs. Gina McCarthy (page 92), an early hire by President Biden – perhaps he heard her *Rethink* essay? – and David Wallace-Wells (page 223) are optimistic about the role an awakened citizenry can play in mitigating these risks. China's announcement, in September 2020, that it would aim to be carbon neutral by 2060, supports such optimism, and is a great leap forward.

For journalists like me who, in 2008, thought the financial crash was the biggest story of their lifetimes, only to confront Brexit, President Trump and Covid-19, recent years have been hard to fathom, let alone explain. To some, all this amounts to a great unravelling, where old certainties disappear and it becomes hard to keep up. But unravelling seems an insufficient metaphor to capture the awesome, terrifying power of what recent years have unleashed. Images of collapsing glaciers and stranded polar bears, or the swift brutality with which the data kings of California can de-platform Donald Trump and his supporters, show that the forces reshaping our world cannot be understood through the familiar categories of yesteryear.

I said that Covid-19 was creating new trends as well as accelerating underlying ones. Among the former is a re-evaluation of cities. Urbanisation – the huge migration of humanity from rural dwellings to the big smoke – has been happening the whole world over for several decades. Might Covid-19 reverse it, at least in the West?

We've all been forced to work from home. Zoom meetings can send you mad, and might well have done; but they are convenient. So too is saving money, and time, on the commute to work. But there is a whiff of snobbery about working from home. It conjures images of a post-lockdown world in which heading downstairs for a turmeric latte is the only interruption to a highly productive eight-hour shift. In truth, 11 per cent of British households have no access to the internet. This rises to a shocking 22 per cent of the poorest households. Moreover, a fifth of all households have no home access to a desktop, laptop or tablet; this rises to 39 per cent of the poorest households.

The pandemic has been much more manageable for those who work with their heads than those who work with their hands. For heart workers – those in health and care professions – it has been exhausting, of course.

Hybrid office and home working is the future. Yet working from home is mainly an option for the rich. According to the *Financial Times*, 'European data suggests three-quarters of jobs in the highest-paying quintile can be done remotely, compared with just 3 per cent of those in the lowest quintile.' The digital divide within countries, as opposed to between them, would be a much bigger political issue if the voice of the poorest were heard more loudly in the media and political debate.

Given that more than half of workers say they would like to work from home some or all the time, the very idea of a city may need to be rethought. It turns out that if you make housing impossibly expensive, and air pollution unbearable, and the cost of transport too high, some people might be put off urban centres. And it turns out that if you can work 5, 10 or 15 miles from the city centre, you can also work 50, 100 and 150 miles away. Londoners bought 73,959 homes outside the city in 2020. That was the highest for four years – despite the fact that the market was shut for nearly two months.

Some cities – notably Cambridge, although it has an unusually fluid and highly skilled population – are undergoing a flip. It used to be with cities that we lived on the outskirts and worked in the middle. In future, might we live and work on the outskirts, and play in the middle? High-street retail, in decline for years, has been devastated by the pandemic, with tens of thousands of stores shut, never to return. Consumption hasn't fallen. It's just moved online.

The crises and horrors of the past have inspired great art and literature. William Shakespeare's entire life was shaped by outbreaks of bubonic plague. Some of his most productive periods, such as 1606–10, coincided with the nastier outbreaks, and the lockdowns associated with them. Thomas Nashe's 'A Litany in Time of Plague' (1593) captures the unrelenting horror of the period, and puts our own in perspective:

> Rich men, trust not in wealth,
> Gold cannot buy you health;
> Physic himself must fade.
> All things to end are made,
> The plague full swift goes by;
> I am sick, I must die.
> Lord, have mercy on us!

T.S. Eliot's *The Waste Land* was written in the shadow of Spanish flu, channelling a similar melancholy to Spengler's *The Decline of the West*. But after them came the Roaring Twenties, and – despite the grim precedent of the Wall Street Crash of 1929 – there are grounds for hope that, in our time, the Roaring 2020s can lift the gloom that Covid-19 has brought.

For an era to bloom, economics and culture must sing together. The huge pent-up savings of consumers across the world may drive a fast economic recovery, though not necessarily one that curbs the inequalities that have grown of late. And while Covid-19 has yet to produce a truly great work of art or literature, there is no good reason to doubt it will. Globally, this is a golden age of film, television, music and storytelling, even if much of it is funded by debt. Culture, that precious fund of emotional knowledge that teaches us not what to think but how to feel; which allows us to transcend our surroundings; and which can connect us to what it is deep and sacred in each other, can flourish in the coming years, but only if enough of us commit to higher ideals of what our public domain should be.

Today, the very idea of our public – that is, shared – space is being reinvented. Centuries ago, it was said that the First Estate was the clergy; the Second, the noblemen (always men, alas); the Third, the middle class; the Fourth, the media. Now we have a Fifth Estate: the internet. It has completely changed the nature of our public domain and created the world's first casually dressed oligarchy. Mostly it has brought convenience and wonder. But it has also brought ruinous misinformation, mobilised hate and fed polarisation. One of our biggest challenges is that today the most important and sensitive topics are being discussed most where they ought to be discussed least: that is, on social media. Those who rightly argue that tabloid newspapers were appallingly hypocritical, cruel and even criminal ought to acknowledge that they also did, and sometimes still do, great journalism, campaigning for the downtrodden and giving a voice to the poor. When Hugh Cudlipp was editor of the *Daily Mirror* in the 1950s, its masthead carried the slogan 'Forward with the People' – unthinkable today. Today, their business model is shattered, and social media is supplanting them. We used to have the gutter press. Now we just have the gutter.

We live in an attention economy. The world's best engineers have designed social media to grab our attention, turning many of us into addicts by often prioritising the outrageous, angry, scary, paranoid and emotional over the cool, calm, clever and kind. In so doing, it has made a few people very rich, and the rest of us disoriented. George Orwell said, 'If you want a picture of the future, imagine a boot stamping on a human face – forever.' The truth might be more mundane. Imagine a thumb, doom-scrolling on Twitter – forever. To adapt Grace Jones, I'm a slave to the algorithm, and so are you.

Western societies are experiencing a profound crisis of connection, in which so-called deaths of despair have risen fast, as life expectancy has fallen. That this should happen even as the internet grows all around us, suggests there are enduring human needs that no digital experience can satisfy. We yearn for love, and harmony between souls. To a much greater extent than is generally recognised, humanity has been hacked. Technology threatens to know us better than we know ourselves. The only answer is an ancient one: time for reflection, contemplation, meditation and above all connection with others is much more important than the dopamine hit of a like or share. Books and radio, even more than film and TV, can provide some of that. I hope *Rethink* does for you.

Another institution that came out of the horror of war and plague is the BBC. Invented to inform, educate and entertain, it has shaped the temper of a people for just short of a century. Today, it exists as a counterpoint to the degradation of our public domain, able to apply scrutiny to power, bring people together, and enlighten our culture. To the extent that *Rethink* has any value, it is precisely to say that at a critical moment in all our lives, there are strong grounds for anxiety; and yet if we only relearn the habit of tolerance, and celebrate curiosity and civility, we might yet shape a world that – against the prevailing winds of change in our time – is better for our children than it was for our parents.

Amol Rajan, London, May 2021

WHO
WE
ARE

CARLO ROVELLI

RETHINKING HUMANITY

As one of the most influential physicists alive today, Carlo Rovelli has achieved acclaim mainly by explaining fields such as quantum gravity and the history of time to lay readers. Here his bewitching gaze turns closer to home.

Rovelli's Seven Brief Lessons on Physics *was an international bestseller. Here he tells a brief version of the tale told in another international bestseller – Yuval Noah Harari's* Sapiens. *That history of our species shows we can choose to tell countless different stories about ourselves. One is of a tribal, brutal ape, who achieves meaning and power through the vanquishing of rivals and outsiders. Yet a happier alternative casts us as the kindest, cleverest species, able to extend our compassion and imagination, and so collaborate. This, Rovelli makes clear, is the difference between civilisation and barbarism. In the post-pandemic world, we need to ensure the better angels of our nature triumph.*

Appeals to the better angels of our nature have led to several stirring books in recent years, from Steven Pinker's

tome with that very name, to economist Rutger Bregman's
Humankind. *Coming from a theoretical physicist, Rovelli's*
essay shows that the yearning to see the best in us, rather than
the worst, is not confined to any intellectual discipline. Indeed,
it's all too human.

This crisis, I think, has been a lesson in humility; it has revealed our fragility. Individually, we have looked into something we usually prefer not to look at much: our mortality. How near can death be? Collectively, we have realised that our powerful, well-organised society is not always so protective, so stable after all. A small virus, little more than a puff of powder, can take many to the grave, leave governments groping in the dark, devastate economies. Humankind is far less master of its own destiny than we believed.

In danger, we human creatures get instinctively closer to one another; we collaborate. This is great. Collaboration is what has made civilisation – but our instinct to collaborate is historically restricted to a family, a group, a company of people, a notion, a country. And historically it has gone hand in hand with conflicts against others. Out of fear, humans unite in tribes and fight other tribes. If this is the reaction triggered by the fear of the pandemic, humankind, I believe, is doomed. This virus is only a forerunner of crises that humankind will have soon to face: climate change, global extinction, mounting worldwide injustice and instability. Only collaboration can navigate us safely through all this.

Past plagues were far more dramatic than this one because all societies faced them alone. We have global science, early warning systems, an ability to share medical equipment, doctors, resources, organisations. One country finds a vaccine, another finds an anti-viral treatment. One can produce the necessary equipment for everybody. Food goes where needed, when needed, and experiences are shared. This is the strength of humankind. The instinct to seek safety in our own country, our own island, our own side, is strong. The temptation to find somebody outside to blame is also strong. I think we must resist it.

We must use our resources to prevent the disasters that nature will certainly bring, to build hospitals and to get organised around the planet. If instead we use our resources to compete, to grow against one another or to build weapons, we are doomed. The future, I believe, depends on how we react to the fear and disruptions of today. If what prevails is isolation and blaming others, humankind marches towards disaster; if we learn from this crisis that our best chances lie in working together around the planet, then the crisis might, after all, help us towards a better future.

RETHINKING POVERTY

After an outspoken attack against a generation of politicians that he calls hypocrites, Pope Francis casts Covid-19 as a potential turning point in history. He says, in words I echoed in the introduction, that what we are experiencing is above all a crisis of connection, so that – even if we don't realise it – we are desperate to reconnect with what matters most. He turns first to nature, arguing that, having lost the 'contemplative dimension' in our lives, we see nature merely as a service to exploit, rather than an inheritance to nourish. And then he turns to the poor. Pope Francis says the poor should be seen not as economic units to be counted, but as noble souls whose dignity has been denied them.

It is worth noting that this is both remarkably outspoken stuff from the head of the Catholic Church, and utterly consistent with his life's work. A humanitarian as much as a religious leader, Jorge Mario Bergoglio has spent decades trying to improve the lot of those enduring penury. Sadly, as our other essayists argue, first the financial crash, and now

Covid-19, have radically worsened inequality – and so make the Pope's argument even more urgent.

This crisis is affecting us all, rich and poor alike, and putting a spotlight on hypocrisy. I am worried by the hypocrisy of certain political personalities who speak of facing up to the crisis, of the problem of hunger in the world, but who, in the meantime, manufacture weapons. This is a time to be converted from this kind of functional hypocrisy. It's a time for integrity. Either we are coherent with our beliefs or we will lose everything.

Every crisis contains both danger and opportunity, the opportunity to move out from the danger. Today, I believe we have to slow down our rate of production and consumption and to learn to understand and contemplate the natural world. We need to reconnect with our real surroundings. This is the opportunity for conversion. I see early signs of an economy that is more human but let us not lose our memory once all this is past, let us not file it away and go back to where we were. This is the time to take the decisive step, to move from using and misusing nature, to contemplating it. We have lost the contemplative dimension and we have to get it back at this time.

And speaking of contemplation, I'd like to dwell on one point: this is the moment to see the poor. Jesus says we will have the poor with us always and that is the truth.

They are a reality we cannot deny but the poor are hidden because poverty is bashful. In Rome, recently, in the midst of the quarantine, a policeman said to a man, 'You can't be on the street, go home.' The response was, 'I have no home, I live in the street.' This pandemic has enabled us to discover such a large number of people who are on the margins and we don't see them because poverty is bashful. They are there but we don't see them because we don't want to see them. They have become part of the landscape, they are things. Saint Teresa of Calcutta saw them and had the courage to embark on a journey of conversion. To see the poor means to restore their humanity. They are not things, not garbage; they are people. We can't settle for a welfare policy such as we have for rescued animals but we often treat the poor like rescued animals. We can't settle for a partial welfare policy.

I am going to dare to offer some advice: this is the time to go to the underground. I am thinking of Dostoevsky's short novel, *Notes from the Underground*. The employees of that prison hospital had become so inured, they treated their poor prisoners like things. And seeing the way they treated one who had just died, the one on the bed alongside tells them, 'Enough. He too had a mother.' We need to tell ourselves this often: that poor person had a mother who raised him lovingly. Later in life, we don't know what happened, but it helps to think of that love he once received through his mother's hope.

We disempower the poor, we don't give them the right to dream of their mothers, they don't know what affection is, many live on drugs. And to see them, to really see them, can help us to discover the piety, the *pietas*, which points towards God and towards our neighbour. Go down into the underground and pass from the hyper-virtual flesh-less world, to the suffering flesh of the poor. This is the conversion we have to undergo. And if we don't start there, it won't happen, it won't happen.

PETER HENNESSY

RETHINKING DEMOCRACY

In his long and much garlanded career, a lot of it spent with the BBC, the historian Peter Hennessy has often asked what we might learn from the experience of another hinge moment: 1945, when an exhausted but victorious Britain launched a new social contract.

As he himself says, comparisons between this pandemic and a six-year war against Nazism are lazy and otiose. But a key, common point was the feeling of national solidarity. The wartime coalition in which Clement Attlee served under Winston Churchill commissioned the seminal and nation-changing Beveridge Report, published in 1942. As Hennessy reminds us, that social analysis was a bestseller, identifying five giants to be vanquished. Looking both backward and forward, Hennessy suggests the five giants of our own time are social care, social housing, technical education, climate change and artificial intelligence. If we learn from history, he suggests, and apply our revived solidarity to practical action, perhaps some good may yet come of the pathogen in our midst.

There had of course been talk of a government of national unity to combat this pandemic, but it hasn't transpired. Instead, we have a prime minister for whom Churchill is a hero, and a Labour leader often compared to Attlee. Which begs the question, if Britain is to defeat the many giant social ills of our time, who will be our Beveridge?

Is it possible that out of our experience of a cruel, capricious and deadly pathogen something of real and enduring value could emerge? That out of tragedy can come possibility and purpose? Is there a usable piece of our past to guide us; to give us hope?

I think there is.

The Covid-19 experience has sharpened our sense of the duty of care we have one for another, that a state has for its people – all of its people – to a degree we have not felt collectively since the Second World War and its aftermath. We heard it week after week on Thursdays at 8pm, as we clapped, cheered and rattled our pots and pans in salute to the NHS frontline and other key workers. It was the sound of people rediscovering themselves.

There are too many differences between six years of total war and the likely length of the Covid emergency for easy comparisons to be made. But what we can learn from those war years is just how powerful and beneficial a 'never again' impulse can be if it is poured into the making of a new deal for the British people.

The great Second World War coalition led by Winston Churchill and Clement Attlee began to plan for exactly that on the back of what was – and still is – the most remarkable report ever produced for a British government. In late 1942, Sir William Beveridge, the leading social arithmetician of his day, identified what he called 'five giants' on the road to recovery and put them in capital letters.

WANT, IGNORANCE, IDLENESS, SQUALOR, DISEASE.

The report was a bestseller.

Beveridge's great insight was that all 'five giants' had to be struck simultaneously if the hard crust of deprivation was to be shattered. After the war, governments of both parties were fuelled by a Beveridge-ite consensus for over 30 years.

Through the grim Covid weeks and months of 2020, can we see the possible outline of a New Beveridge, a post-corona banner we can all rally round – a banner emblazoned with the heraldry of a new consensus?

We can. I think there is a hard-edged, not a fudged consensus to be crafted using five priorities:

- Social care; something must be done and fast
- A big public/private push on social housing
- Getting technical education right at last after 150 years of trying

- Combatting and mitigating climate change
- Preparing our country and our people for the full impact of artificial intelligence on our productive capacity and our society

If our politicians could pick up this new consensus and run with it – finding the right tone and pitch of language in which to convey it – the early 2020s could be one of the most creative and productive patches of our history and a worthy memorial to the Covid fallen.

It has taken a pathogen for us to find and refresh our shared duty of care. But rediscover it we have.

ANAND GIRIDHARADAS

RETHINKING CAPITALISM

There are several reasons that Anand Giridharadas has become a bestselling author and leading voice of liberal America, beyond any plausibility of his arguments. One is that his appearance is striking, with his long, spiky grey hair. Another is that his most recent book, Winners Take All, *is an attack on what he sees as the hypocrisy of super-rich elites who trumpet their philanthropy while paying little tax.*

Yet another is that he used to work at McKinsey, those high priests of modern capitalism, and therefore has some inside knowledge of how today's rich obtain and retain their wealth. And then there is the alluring simplicity of an argument that comes close to saying – but doesn't quite go this far – that, when you look at all the interlocking crises of our time, you might think money is at the root of all evil.

Like the French economist Thomas Piketty, Giridharadas argues that democracies in the West have failed to rein in the worst excesses of capitalism. His suggestion that the killing of black men by American police is itself a kind of virus is powerful. And in recognising that, for all the misery it has caused, Covid-19 has brought a 'strange gift', which is the revelation that we can't go on like this, our essayist finds a reason to be grateful amid the gloom.

You and I live in a grim time. But it is a special kind of grim time that happens every so often in history, a grim time pregnant with hope. What I see in my country, America, is an old society dying and a new society panging to be born. With the birth of a child, you pray, but with the birth of a new country, you choose. We must choose the next country. They say it is easier to see things with 20-20 hindsight, but when we look back on this time, we may remember the terrible year that gave us 20-20 foresight instead. A year that allowed us to see more clearly than before what we were allowing ourselves to become and to choose other roads and other songs.

America is living not through one crisis but at least five. The pandemic and the already unhealthy host society the virus attacked. The employment crisis unleashed by that pandemic, that pushed our inequitable economy from chronically ill to terminally diseased. The racial crisis fuelled by police barbarism and institutionalised hatred. The democratic crisis embodied, but hardly initiated, by a mad demagogue in the highest office in the land (at the time of writing), who behaves more and more like a fascist. And the environmental crisis, hovering over the others, threatening everything that breathes. These are distinct crises but they intersect. The pandemic wouldn't have killed so many if, early on, more people in America could have taken a day of paid sick leave when they felt unwell. The democratic crisis is the fruit of many white people preferring to surrender the rule of law and decency than to surrender their own privileges. The climate crisis is what it is because the democracy is in no position to do anything. The cries of Black Lives Matter are a response to police abuses but they speak, as well, of a virus that took far more black lives than white lives as a percentage of the population.

It can be depressing and intimidating to see the crises this way. But then, I think, that were it not for the enormity and the simultaneity of these crises, we would never escape them. These synched crises have freed us from any illusion that we may have been living right. They make plain that we will either transform our way of life or we will decline and fall, as Americans and possibly as a species. They have given us a strange gift. The knowledge that returning, going back to normal, is impossible, that our choices now are imagination or death.

So now we see the future with 20-20 foresight. It is plain as day now that the capitalism we were practising would soon have destroyed us. Plain as day that America will never be whole, so long as white domination is the law and the culture. It is plain now that any of us is only as healthy as the most precariously insured, least well-tended member of the society. It is plain that a society built on extraction from the planet will eventually extract us too. Plain that oligarchy is still oligarchy and feudalism is still feudalism, even when they are reincarnated with corporate social responsibility, philanthropy and woke social media posts. Imagining and building and organising and electing this new society into being is the work of our time. It is not easy work, for the faint of heart. But with 20-20 foresight, we can see that there is another way of life, another social order, another way of relating to each other, another way of living with and on our planet, another way of judging what matters, that these things glimmer on the horizon. With 20-20 foresight, let us march towards these things.

JARED DIAMOND

RETHINKING A GLOBAL RESPONSE

Jared Diamond is one of those intellectuals that you always want to hear, on pretty much every subject, and not just because of his marvellous Bostonian accent. The author of Guns, Germs and Steel *knows a thing or two about pandemics. In fact, he knows a lot more than that. He asks us to Rethink A Global Response.*

In this moving essay, Diamond, who is 82, makes clear how his life has been tragically touched by Covid-19. This sombre beginning informs the rest of his argument, in which he puts the first global pandemic for a century in its proper context. That is to say, without giving too much away, that if you think beating this dastardly pathogen is a challenge – one that has strained global alliances to breaking point, and impoverished hundreds of millions of people – wait until you comprehend what's needed to beat climate change. We have closed societies and economies across the world to save ourselves from this invisible killer. Why haven't we done the same to stop global heating, whose horrific effects are visible to anyone who cares to look?

The biggest legacy of coronavirus will also be the most sinister: a fundamental change in the relationship between the citizen and the state. During the pandemic, the state exercised coercive power over its citizens on a scale never previously attempted. It took effective legal control, enforced by the police, over the personal lives of the entire population: where they could go, whom they could meet, what they could do. It placed them all under a form of house arrest, qualified only by their right to do a limited number of things approved by ministers. It was the most significant interference with personal freedom in the history of our country, the abandonment of a tradition of liberty going back three centuries.

How might Covid-19 cause our world to change for the better? Your first reaction to that question is likely to be: what an obscene idea! How could a disease that kills people and that is shattering our economies create a better world? That's certainly my own strong reaction, because my wife and I are still in a state of shock from the deaths of four of our closest friends in the last few weeks, friends whom we had treasured for 50 or 60 years. Yes, it's indeed an obscene idea today to look for any good in Covid. But what will the world be like, when we have vaccines against it?

The unique thing about Covid is that, for the first time in world history, people everywhere are being forced to recognise that all of us face a global problem demanding a global solution. Jet planes guarantee that no country can solve its Covid problem by itself. As long as the virus exists anywhere in the world, any country that temporarily eliminates it within its borders will just get reinfected by travellers from other countries that haven't eliminated it, as happened in New Zealand. We recognise Covid as a problem because it kills its victims within a week or two, and there is no doubt that they died of Covid. But even in the worst-case scenario, Covid will kill only a few tens of millions of the world's 7.7 billion people, and economies will recover.

That makes Covid a minor problem, compared to the three really big global problems that kill people slowly and unspectacularly, and that have threatened to destroy our economies forever. You all know what those three problems are. They are climate change, unsustainable use of world resources, and the consequences of inequality among the world's peoples. But we haven't mounted global responses to those really big problems in the way that we now are mounting a global response to Covid. Why not? It's obvious. It's because climate change kills us and ruins our economies much more slowly and subtly than does Covid. And so it hasn't commanded our urgent attention.

But climate change, like Covid, demands a global response. Winds mix carbon dioxide, CO_2, in the atmosphere, just as jet planes mix the Covid virus around the world. No country can reduce its own atmospheric CO_2 and protect itself against climate change as long as CO_2 levels are rising in the atmosphere over the rest of the world. Covid, and our global war against it, are teaching us a lesson. And so, I hope that, once our global response to Covid starts to defeat it, we shall thereby learn, finally, how to mount global responses to climate change and to those other really big global threats. If that happens, then Covid's tragedy may have caused our world to change for the better.

ZIAUDDIN SARDAR

RETHINKING NORMALITY

Of all the phrases that have found a new and more comfortable berth in our language, perhaps "the new normal" is the one that conceals the most and says the least. But what does it conceal, exactly?

At base, normality means the thing that connects yesterday with today. That implies a degree of continuity. Yet as I noted in the Introduction, this is the age of History's great acceleration, in which change is the only constant. If things are changing so fast, then it follows that the continuity we take for granted, the feeling of a reliable normality, is itself an illusion. The 'new normal' implies there was an 'old normal.' But the old normal was in such a state of flux that it could hardly be relied on. Perhaps the new normal will also turn out to be an illusion.

As Sardar eloquently makes clear, there are patterns and habits from the life before Covid-19 that will not, and cannot, be part of the post-pandemic world. When people talk of a new normal, what they're really saying is that we can't carry on like this. It then behoves them to explain which bit of 'this' is unsustainable, just as Sardar did.

The pandemic has announced a new beginning. The beginning of post-normal times. It's a time when little out there can be trusted or gives us confidence, a time of accelerating change, of uncertainty, indecision, social and cultural upheaval, and realignment of power. We are now living in an in-between period where old orthodoxies and established ways of thinking and doing are dying, new ones have yet to be born, and very few things seem to make sense. We are dangerously hanging between the no longer and the not yet.

So, welcome to post-normal times.

It's time to grow up and forget about returning to normal because normal was the problem in the first place. Rather than teaching us anything new, the pandemic forces us to look in the mirror. But can we accept what looks back at us?

What we see is that we live in an interconnected, interdependent, complex world full of contradictions. In a rapidly changing environment, complexity and contradictions generate positive feedback that leads quickly to chaos. We can expect more chaotic occurrences, more pandemics, more extreme weather events, more economic turbulence, and more social and cultural upheaval. That is going to be the new reality.

Societies collapse for many reasons such as resource depletion and environmental change but complexity is an essential element. As societies become more and more complex, they reach a point of diminishing returns; things fall apart and collapse follows. And it does look like we are following in the footsteps of the Mayans, the Aztec and the Roman Empire. This is the proverbial chickens of western civilisation coming home to roost.

There is a key difference. Earlier collapses were regional. Western civilisation is now a global civilisation. It has overstepped planetary boundaries, of which climate change is only one indicator. So if the western civilisation goes down, it can take all of us with it and destroy the planet in the process.

It is thus in all our interest, no matter who and where we are, to adjust to the new reality of post-normal times.

In the short term, this means we need to learn to appreciate complexity. Accept the fact that complex problems require complex solutions, and there are no simple, quick answers to anything. We must embrace uncertainty as uncertainty will be the new norm. And, as contradictions cannot be resolved, we will need to learn to transcend contradictions. We need to recognise that our ignorance increases with every advance in knowledge. We thus have to learn to live with increasing ignorance.

But in the long term we need to slow down. Abandon the long cherished ideal of growth, the ideology of the cancer cell. We need to return to planetary boundaries and that demands degrowth. Degrowth requires us to rethink ourselves – our devastating industrial agriculture, caustic factory farming, continuous harmful developments, our relationship with nature, our lifestyles and desires, what we eat and what we wear, our ways of being, knowing and doing – the whole damn lot.

It really is time to move on from the nostalgia for life before the lockdown.

RETHINKING ANCIENT WISDOM

Highly alert as he is to the present threats to humanity, particularly that of climate change, the Dalai Lama here describes a checklist of priorities for the post-pandemic world. I was taken aback by the political bite of his message, wrapped in compassion though it may be.

His emphasis on the ancient ways of the old masters of the East, who saw History and Humanity through a less teleological lens than the Abrahamic faiths did, appealed to this son of India very much. The mysticism and transcendental power of Eastern thought has often appealed to a minority of Westerners, many of them artistic, and several of them far from sober during the 1960s. Half a century on, as the world re-balances towards Asia, the ruling philosophies of the East will find ways to impress themselves further on the imaginations of people all around the globe.

Another moment from his essay that jumped out at me is when he implies that ancient Indian knowledge would be a more significant player in the modern world if rapacious

Britishers hadn't repressed so much of it under the cloak of their civilising, imperial mission. In addressing the complex imperial heritage that is so much a part of our cultural conversation, the Dalai Lama's contribution to Rethink *pulled off a rare trick. It was both timely and timeless.*

Maybe the one small contribution I can make is to remind all our neighbours on this blue planet to utilise the human brain effectively. We are the only animals that have a discerning mind, so it is up to us to use it constructively. Therefore, I am always stressing education, and our potential for thinking more about humanity.

If we can use our intelligence properly, and combine it with realistic, clear-sighted moral thinking, then I think that within the next decades or so, there is real potential for growth, for progress. After that, if global warming makes our planet uninhabitable, we will have to go to some other planet – not by spacecraft, but by spirit!

I always tell people that now I have four basic commitments. The first is the promotion of the oneness of all human beings. I am just one of 7 billion beings on this planet and we all share the same hopes, the same fears, the same potential for compassion. My second commitment is the promotion of religious harmony. So many different traditions have arisen across the world, each with its own philosophy and history. But all of them carry the same message for love, so there is always potential for harmony.

My third commitment is to the preservation of Tibetan culture – a unique language and tradition and heritage that, I think, can contribute something to all humanity. I It is also critical that we protect the very special ecology of Tibet, from which most of the great rivers of Asia originate, and work to keep the entire Tibetan plateau green. And my fourth commitment is to the revival of ancient Indian knowledge. Great Indian thinkers have promoted the concepts of *ahimsa*, non-violence, and *karuna*, compassion, for thousands of years. But unlike religious beliefs these principles have universal and logical appeal as well as practical benefit to all, whether one is a believer or non-believer. They are a fundamental expression of secular ethics. If people paid more attention to these ideas in their day-to-day lives, the world would be a better place.

We often speak about the importance of physical hygiene for our well-being. We also need to cultivate emotional hygiene, too, using our minds to tackle destructive emotions and achieve peace of mind. I really feel that all of us can gain from paying more attention to India's rich and unique thousand-year tradition of working with the emotions and the mind. If the educational systems of the twenty-first century can combine the study of the world of matter with the study of the mind, I think we can all be happier and healthier human beings.

C.K. Lᴀʟ

RETHINKING INSTITUTIONS

C.K. Lal is a great eminence in literary and journalistic circles of the Indian sub-continent. Nepalese by origin, and also an engineer, his essay is broad in scope, but can ultimately be distilled to one, grand theme.

A reconsideration of institutions, and the role they play in public life, has long been brewing. In the UK, the Conservative intellectual David Willetts wrote an influential pamphlet for the Social Market Foundation in 1994, called Civic Conservatism. *It said that politics had become so distracted by the autonomy of the individual on the one hand, and the power and efficacy of the State on the other, that it had ignored the supreme importance of what was in between. Some people call this society, others community, others family. Willetts ran with institutions, broadly defined, from local associations to domestic institutions such as marriage.*

New Labour adopted some of his ideas; Prime Minister David Cameron's Big Society accepted virtually all of them. In this essay, Lal argues that it is the institutions in our life, the domestic, local and municipal, that will need to be re-engi-neered to forge the best possible post-pandemic world.

Pre-Covid, bigger was better. Post-Covid, will Schumacher's forgotten formulation, that small is beautiful, find a new life? Science has failed to offer immediate solutions for what was being termed as a little flu. As I write in summer 2020, the prospect of curative treatment or preventive vaccine looks far away. When science fails, people look for solace in religion. This time, even gods and goddesses abandoned their faithful. Doors of churches, mosques, temples and prayer halls were shut for seekers. People then asked the state, why are people dying? Why the shortage of basic safety kits such as PPEs and even surgical masks for doctors, nurses, caregivers and cleaners on the frontline? It wasn't rocket science to produce a life-support system, and it wouldn't have cost as much as an expedition to Mars to provide hospitals with sufficient ventilators. In the absence of adequate and timely response, faith in the government hit an all-time low. Markets proved to be bigger truants; the supply-side for basic drugs such as paracetamol, used for body ache and fever, and hydroxychloroquine, primary treatment for malaria, which mosquitoes transmit, failed to match the demand.

Ditched by the state, and disappointed with the forces of the market, people began to return to the community.

The civil society, however, had lost its soul in the wake of globalisation. Charity was an industry, and social service was no longer a vocation and had become a profession. Cracks in the family, one of the earliest and most basic institutions of human civilisation, began to appear bigger when looked at from close quarters. The lockdown exposed inequality in the institution of marriage. Despite decades of progress, women are still required to work longer hours. The demand for childcare, when day-care centres were closed, made many youngsters, some of them staying with their parents, reconsider their plans for marriage and rethink the supposed pleasures of parenthood.

Post-Covid, there'll be less reliance on the ability of science to answer all questions. The realisation that life has to be endured, rather than conquered, should make the world a little less competitive. The small state, the so-called night watchman, was caught napping on duty. The leviathan was unable to move. The principle of subsidiarity, which entails empowering municipal governments, had failed to find traction for decades. Now even sub-municipal units have higher acceptability. From aiming to be global players, the markets will have to go local. Smaller community organisations rather than giant professional bodies, or International Non-Governmental Organisations (INGOs), will begin to attract fresh adherents. Survival of the family will depend upon the ability of men to be equal partners at home. The HIV

AIDS scare had strengthened long-term partnerships, even if not marriage per se. The Covid-19 pandemic will probably make individuals rethink the purpose of life. If procreation isn't the primary responsibility of a person, the institution of marriage will lose one of its main justifications. Freed from institutional constraints of religion, science, state, market, civil society and the family, individuals will redesign the post-Covid world with the person at the centre of smaller units. Hopefully human concerns will triumph over property rights.

Jarvis Cocker

RETHINKING AN ENVIRONMENTAL REVOLUTION

Who, ultimately, has responsibility for overcoming climate change? Is it governments? Businesses? Engineers? Or perhaps, to coin a phrase, it's us: the common people.

Jarvis Cocker, lead singer in the band Pulp, grapples with this question not through the prism of policy, with its trade-offs and need for consensus, but through awe at the beauty and loyalty of nature, and in particular birdsong. So many of us have, as he notes, been mesmerised and even reassured by nature rushing in to fill the social and professional void in our lives. Might love of dense woodland, distant hills and – as you'll hear – the song of the hen harrier, be enough to awake in us a new consciousness of our duty as stewards of the Earth?

Cocker argues that reversing ecological catastrophe, which is not just imminent but already all around us, requires something like a reawakening among us all.

Turnip Townshend's real name, by the way, was Charles. He was a viscount, and brother-in-law of Robert Walpole, Britain's

first prime minister. An unlikely revolutionary, you might think;
but then so too is the persuasive former lead singer of Pulp.

Turnip Townshend, a name to conjure with, a name not to be forgotten in a hurry. I stopped studying history at school at the age of 14 but I still remember Turnip Townshend and his Norfolk rotation. I found myself thinking about him lately, during the lockdown. Let me try to explain why.

One thing a lot of people seemed to agree was a silver lining during the lockdown, was the way that nature immediately rushed in to fill the gap left by the lack of human activity. You no longer had to tune into Radio 4's *Tweet of the Day* to hear wild bird calls; they were all around us. The most haunting sound I heard during the confinement was the call of a hen harrier in a nearby field while I was on a walk. Usually, hen harriers are only seen on remote moorland, whereas this was next to a normally busy road. I'd say it was 'unprecedented', if I wasn't so heartily sick of hearing that word.

And all over the world, there were similar reports: people marvelling at mountain goats roaming the streets of Llandudno, Wales, raccoons frolicking in Central Park, New York, fallow deer grazing in the residential streets of Harold Hill, east London, dolphins in the canals of Venice ... (Yeah, okay, I know that last one didn't really happen but it's such a nice idea.) I guess we noticed because we *could* notice. The background noise of road traffic and planes flying overhead was absent. But also because, after years of dire warnings on the effects of climate change, we wanted to notice. We so wanted nature to make this spectacular comeback.

One argument that certainly won't be coming back any time soon after lockdown is the one that claims human activity has no marked effect on the environment. Really? Everyone but everyone noticed that marked effect when we were forced to surrender the stage for a couple of months. It's as clear as day: our actions sure as hell do have consequences. Similarly, that old B-movie-esque trope that technology and science will step in at the 11th hour to pull us back from the brink of global disaster has been given the lie by this pandemic. At the time of writing (May 2020), the considered opinion is that we are still many months away from a vaccine and that's with all the best scientific minds in the world working on the same problem. A quick, last-minute fix for the environment just isn't going to happen.

Which brings me back to my old mate, Turnip Townshend. His name will live forever because he kickstarted the agricultural revolution. His Norfolk rotation involved farmers leaving one field fallow every year (fallow except for growing yummy turnips, that is), hence his nickname. The fields took it in turns to be fallow – that's the rotation part.

So how's about an environmental revolution? Rotating fallow years for the planet. We've seen the effect just a couple of months can have: imagine what six months or a whole year could do. Imagine. And I'm not suggesting we all stay at home again, watching Netflix and doing online quizzes for the duration either. Set folks to work on environmental projects, like the mass insulation initiative about to take place in Germany. Or the rewilding of former industrial sites. It seems the received wisdom that there'll be a fair amount of surplus workforce sloshing around in the wake of this crisis. Use it. People need to work, give them work they can be proud of, that we can all be proud of. And then the name of Turnip Townshend will echo through the land once more, accompanied by the unforgettable song of the hen harrier.

CLARE CHAMBERS

RETHINKING THE BODY

Never before in human history have we been so bombarded by images of idealised beauty, or had such freedom – through digital technology – to advertise a false picture of ourselves. We can hope that the epidemic of anxiety and other, darker maladies this has led to will be vanquished in the post-pandemic world.

For many of us, the philosopher Clare Chambers notes, life in lockdown has changed our relationship with our bodies. We are intensely conscious of our physical fragility in the face of this invisible pathogen. At the same time, access to facilities designed to improve our appearance – the hairdressers, barbers and beauticians – has been denied. We've allowed our hair to grow and grey, and there is relief from the sheer exhaustion of being forever on display. And yet, as Chambers argues, young people, for whom life is ever more online, are pulled by algorithms and self-consciousness towards projecting a false picture of themselves. That is: lying. We are all advertisers now. In a better world, she asks, how might we emancipate young people from the burdens and anguish of life as an eternal exhibition?

Chambers is right: the selfie is the digital pinnacle of a culture of objectification, in which we are judged not by our actions or sentiments, but by our sartorial flotsam. And that's no way to judge people at all.

The pandemic focuses our minds on our bodies. It makes us profoundly aware that we rely on our bodies working well: on our heart's beat, on our blood's flow, on our lungs' breath. It forces us to acknowledge the fragility of function.

In normal times, many of us focus more on how our bodies *look* than how they *work*. Cosmetic surgery has become a mainstream practice, with new cosmetic procedures constantly being developed. Psychologists diagnose an epidemic of appearance-related anxiety. The 2019 girls' attitudes survey found that the top three pressures faced online by British girls aged 11 to 16 were 'to look pretty all the time', 'to get more likes', and 'to have a picture-perfect life'.

Will Covid-19 disrupt these worries about how we look? Might it push us into valuing how our bodies feel from the inside? Could it let us care more about our health than our beauty?

One theme of lockdown has been what to wear. A Japanese company made the news for its 'work from home pyjamas': comfy loungewear beneath, a formal shirt from the mid chest up – the only part visible when video conferencing. Many of us are selecting our comfiest clothes, freed from the tyranny of the work uniform or the office dress code. During lockdown, we find out where in our wardrobe our real friends are.

Do you find that the clothes you're wearing to stay at home are very different from the clothes you used to wear? Has your perspective shifted from outward appearance to inner comfort? Do you normally dress to please others, whereas now you need only please yourself? Does this feel liberating?

Or are you dressing much the same as usual? Is that because you always dress for comfort, wearing the clothes that feel good to you? Or is it because your external appearance is still fundamental to your sense of self? Does looking good make you feel better?

Contemporary culture encourages us to objectify each other and also to objectify ourselves. When we objectify ourselves, we focus on how we look to others and how we compare to others. We think primarily about how we appear rather than how we feel.

This self-objectification reaches its pinnacle with the selfie, the photograph we take of ourselves and then post online for others' approval. The selfie enables us to objectify ourselves in the most direct sense, because we can take our image and manipulate it digitally. Over 70 per cent of girls filter the images they post online. We create the image we think others want to see.

Lockdown offers us the chance to escape constant surveillance. It offers a period of invisibility, a space where we are not always on display. It offers an excuse for letting ourselves go, letting the grey show, letting the hair grow, letting the diet go. It lets us experiment, to find out which things we do to our bodies make us feel good and which don't. Were our beauty practices really for ourselves, or were they for others after all?

We long for life to get back to normal, to have the luxury of worrying more about our looks than our lives. But how will the virus affect our attitudes to our bodies? When our social interactions are almost entirely online, the pull of the image may become even stronger.

We can continue to curate and enhance our virtual image, editing and refining it before we present it to the world. But perhaps the pandemic will situate us firmly in our bodies as biological and material things, emphasising their health and their function as their fundamental value. Perhaps the virus could pull us back from the appearance-obsessed visual culture that has caused so much harm to our mental health.

STEVEN PINKER

RETHINKING HUMAN NATURE

Many people who involve themselves in politics or public disputes of any kind are arguing, even when they don't realise it, about the Enlightenment. That magnificent chapter in the history of our species unleashed a cognitive revolution that led to the development of industries and cultures through science, engineering and invention.

Pinker's most recent book, Enlightenment's Wake, *which I interviewed him about, is a blizzard of data that shows how, on countless measures across health and wealth, we sapiens have improved our lot. For Pinker, this constitutes progress. On the other side of the argument are people like the philosopher John Gray, for whom progress is a secular delusion. Champions of progress, Gray believes, merely accept the premise of the Abrahamic faiths, that human history is a moral drama whose final act is salvation. Whereas material knowledge, also called science, is cumulative, moral knowledge is not. Far from saving us, science will never deliver us from the reality of human nature. I put these two positions to you at length because, as you read Pinker, you might want to consider which side you are on.*

And me? Well, since you ask, I reckon the point about the Enlightenment is not just that we owe it so much. It's that we're due another one.

Many people have trouble reconciling the fact of human progress – that we have become healthier, richer, safer and smarter – with the constraints of human biology. Many idealists resist the very idea that evolution shaped the mind, because it would seem to suggest that progress is impossible – after all, 'you can't change human nature'. Many cynics, all too happy to deny progress, feel vindicated by the pandemic, because it shows that life has gotten not better but worse.

But these are misconceptions of human nature *and* human progress. What makes humans unusual is a triad of faculties: know-how, which allows us to understand and manipulate the world; language, which allows us to pool these ideas; and sociality, which impels us to cooperate with our fellows.

Among the brainchildren of these faculties are the printed and electronic word, and the institutions of science and governance, which allow knowledge to accumulate over generations. When people use knowledge to improve their lives, retaining the innovations that work, the result is progress.

That's *all* that progress consists of; it is not some mystical force that carries us ever upwards. On the contrary, the forces of nature tend to grind us down, including the inexorable increase in disorder, and the conflicts built into the evolutionary process.

Among these hazards is infectious disease. Our bodies are irresistible targets for exploitation by smaller and faster-evolving organisms. From a germ's point of view, you are a big yummy mound of gingerbread, there for the eating.

So all organisms have evolved defences against being devoured from the inside, including sexual reproduction and our immune systems.

And we humans have evolved another weapon against pathogens: our cognitive, social and linguistic faculties. It is *these* adaptations that led to the recent conquest of the infectious diseases that felled our ancestors in horrendous numbers. They allowed us to discover vaccination, sanitation, antibiotics and other advances in public health and medicine that dramatically extended life expectancy starting two centuries ago.

So it is no refutation of the idea of progress that another pathogen has launched an offensive against us – that is in the nature of life. Yet the biology of *Homo sapiens* gives us good reasons to expect that the disease will be subdued in its turn: not as an inevitable step in some march of progress, but if (and only if) we redouble the commitment, which human evolution enables but does not guarantee, to the application of scientific knowledge to improve human wellbeing.

TOM RIVETT-CARNAC

RETHINKING HISTORY

Something very, very profound is happening all around us. Our history – the collective story, or stories, we tell about our heritage – is being contested, claimed and reclaimed as never before. Suddenly history itself is the battlefield. Statues toppled, curricula torn up, common orthodoxies shattered. For many people, this is hugely unsettling, and understandably so. When the stories we tell ourselves and each other, about ourselves and each other, are edited or rewritten, it can shake our souls to their core. For others, this is a chance to be intellectually ambitious in public life; to give a fuller, franker account of who we are and how we got here. One person in the latter camp is the climate change campaigner Tom Rivett-Carnac.

As Rivett-Carnac makes clear, this battle is personal. His ancestors did things in what was euphemistically called the Raj that he, today, cannot countenance or ignore. But in his telling of it, this is not a burden to apologise for. After all, he wasn't there to cast his verdict at the time. Rather, the past, for good and for ill, is something to be understood, as a spur to action today.

History is an infinite selection of narratives that compete and coalesce. Our work in writing it is never done. Or as the novelist William Faulkner put it, 'The past is never dead. It's not even past.'

The Covid-19 pandemic has laid bare both how interconnected the human family has become and also the reality that some groups among us are disproportionately vulnerable and suffer more than they should. What's more, the murder of George Floyd and the resultant outcry about persistent racial injustice has shown us that often the reason those groups are disproportionately vulnerable is historical. And with that awakening has come an opening; an opportunity to re-examine our history with new eyes and provide us with a more honest platform on which to build our future.

Re-examining history is something I know a little about. When I was growing up, my grandfather would talk during long winter evenings in his woodshop about the years of service our forebears had put into what was still in those days called the colonies. Indeed, Rudyard Kipling wrote in 1897 that if there was one loaf of bread left in India, the Rivett-Carnac family would be entitled to fully a quarter of it. Those were the stories I grew up on and nothing I learned in school dislodged them, so it wasn't until I was a young man standing in a dusty, formerly grand art gallery in northern India that I learned that the East India Company – of which my direct fore-bear was chairman and which many of my ancestors served – had actually deposed, plundered, murdered and usurped through a rapacious system of exploitation. The 'story of glory', of riches and rewards for some, was one of misery, servitude and exploitation for many others.

Now it is a fact that, however I may feel about it, I can do nothing to change the actions of my forebears centuries later. But I do have a responsibility to retell that brutal history without pretence of virtue. Doing other-wise would be an act of narrative violence towards those who were persecuted and would also deny the reality that that history still shapes our world today in ways we do not think about enough. My history is just an extreme version of many of our histories. We need to face it for both deep moral reasons but also because it is not just about what happened in the past. It is also about what needs to happen now.

The global pandemic has shown us, perhaps more starkly than ever before, that this human story is now so inextricably linked together, so interdependent, that none of us can hive ourselves away and protect ourselves from the fate of all of us. That fact means we must face the great perils of the future together and to realise that moving beyond injustice, restoring nature, eliminating racism and solving the climate crisis can only be achieved if we recognise that they are all fundamentally the same challenge of how humans live well together on this earth.

I have chosen to spend my life working on the climate crisis. But I do so due to a commitment to social justice. The issues are all interconnected and all of us – every individual, every company, every nation – has a role to play through deeds and values to face this while we can, since if we lose control of the climate, the future will be one of injustice and inequality and loss of dignity.

We have a choice. We either keep perpetuating the myths we've become used to telling about our history, as the world is torn apart by widening injustices, future pandemics and unmitigated climate change. Or we can start building for a future for all of us, based on an honest retelling of history that gives us a chance to not remain trapped in the echoes of the past, but to build a 'new normal' one where we can either all rise or fall together as we emerge from this and look to the future.

I am struck by the thought that, if I'm lucky, one day I will share stories with my own grandchildren. The family history they will learn will be a more complex one than I heard. But along with dark chapters I hope to share stories of how in the end, perhaps in the aftermath of this pandemic, we faced the demons of the past and, with that courage, embraced the infinite possibility of a shared bright future that is still ours to choose.

JONATHAN SUMPTION

RETHINKING
THE STATE

It was Thomas Hobbes, the natural scientist (as they called men of his ilk in the mid-seventeenth century), who essentially founded modern politics with his great work Leviathan. *The key feature of Hobbes's Leviathan – the modern state – is its doubleness: coercion and consent. It has coercive power over the citizen, which the citizen willingly gives up in order to be more secure and more free. This pandemic has seen Hobbes's Leviathan flourish across the globe.*

As befits a former British Supreme Court justice, Sumption is very precise in his language; and it's important that he be represented fairly. He is no Hobbesian, in the sense of endorsing Hobbes's analysis; indeed he describes Hobbes as sinister. Yet Sumption makes clear that we are all Hobbesian, because Hobbes laid out the dilemmas of the state clearly, and our politics largely exists within a paradigm he described. We all have to think, every day, of the tension between freedom and security.

Freedom was the great ideological victor of the twentieth century. After two horrific wars, it triumphed over rival

totalitarianisms. Recently, however, there has been a commu-
nitarian correction in our politics, and the libertarian impulse
– always more popular in the USA than in Britain – has
begun to go out of fashion. According to the emerging British
consensus, freedom has huge value; but so too do belonging,
solidarity and much else, including security. Liberalism's
over-reach, on this analysis, is that it prioritised liberty at the
expense of those other sentiments.

The great value of Sumption's essay is that it reminds us of
the immense value of freedom, and argues that it should not
be sacrificed too readily. Across the globe, the pandemic has led
to a sudden enlargement of the State, both economically and
in terms of the power granted to authorities to deprive us of
freedom. You don't have to be a lockdown sceptic to wonder
if this has gone too far. Or to fear that, if the State grows too
powerful, something precious will be lost to all of us.

The biggest legacy of coronavirus will also be the most
sinister: a fundamental change in the relationship
between the citizen and the state. During the pandemic,
the state exercised coercive power over its citizens on a
scale never previously attempted. It took effective legal
control, enforced by the police, over the personal lives of
the entire population: where they could go, whom they
could meet, what they could do. It placed them all under
a form of house arrest, qualified only by their right to do
a limited number of things approved by ministers. It was

the most significant interference with personal freedom in the history of our country, the abandonment of a tradition of liberty going back three centuries.

The most significant thing about it was that, at least initially, it was welcomed by the great majority of the population. The reason was that they were afraid, and fear is the most potent instrument of the absolute state. It is the most effective and economical way of inducing compliance, short of actual force. Experience suggests that people who are sufficiently afraid will voluntarily surrender their liberty.

The capacity of the state to apply coercion has immeasurably increased over the past century and a half. This is the result, partly of the expanded machinery of bureaucratic enforcement, and partly of technological changes which have greatly increased the state's ability to access and retrieve information.

What the state can do, sooner or later it will do. People demand that this great plenitude of power should be used for purposes of which they approve. In a world where people are no longer willing to accept risk or tolerate misfortune, they approve of almost anything that they believe will increase their security. There is an irony at the heart of these instincts. People distrust the motives of politicians. But they have unbounded confidence, which no amount of experience will dent, in the benign power of the state to protect them against an ever-wider range of risks.

The great seventeenth-century philosopher Thomas Hobbes believed that people voluntarily, but entirely and irrevocably, surrender their freedom to an absolute state, in exchange for security. In the last six months, the British people have been acting out this sinister image. When personal security prevails over every other value, personal liberty becomes little more than the gift of tyrants.

WHAT
WE DO

DAVID SKELTON

RETHINKING INDUSTRY

Here's a prediction for the post-pandemic world: we'll see a fundamental rebalancing in our societies, and by extension our economies, between head, heart and hand. As the author David Goodhart has argued, for most of the post-war period, societies everywhere have upheld cognitive skill as the gold standard of human capability, and the route to success in our age of achievement. The education that we encourage is all about brain power. And cognitive skill, especially through the tech and finance sectors, is the surest route to wealth. Is that healthy?

This pandemic has reminded us that other types of human endeavour should be better rewarded. We applaud key workers, but their pay and social status is far below that of people who move money around. Increasing their pay might mean higher taxes, but it would recognise labours of the heart – that is, caring. You know, the sorts of jobs robots will never do. As for labours of the hand – manufacturing – a revival could be good for our wallets, high streets and souls.

David Skelton's book Little Platoons *is a Burkean cry for politics to revive small communities, many of which have been emaciated by globalisation. As he notes, industry isn't just about generating material wealth, or money; it's also about moral wealth, or love.*

The UK's Covid experience has illustrated why we need to reindustrialise our economy and why we need to value economic resilience as much as we value efficiency. Community bonds have been strengthened over the past few months and we need to maintain that increased sense of community. Almost a million people volunteered to help the NHS and this has reminded us that there is such a thing as society and it's stronger than ever. But we've also seen elements of our life and our economy that we really need to improve and many of these problems have been caused by the decline of manufacturing industry. Too many so-called post-industrial parts of the country, which once relied on manufacturing jobs, have seen workers shift from proud, skilled work, to low-paid, low-skilled, insecure work. This kind of low-paid work has left people more exposed to both the health and the financial impacts of Covid.

The Office for National Statistics has said that Covid has had a more severe impact on deprived communities, with the mortality rate in the most-deprived areas being more than double that in the least-deprived areas. Other research has found that these post-industrial towns are among the hardest hit by the virus and its economic aftermath. Industrial decline hasn't just impacted those places that once depended on manufacturing jobs, it's also made our economy less productive, less resilient and less able to mobilise quickly in times of great crisis. The large countries who have responded most quickly and most successfully to Covid, notably Germany and South Korea, are also those countries that have maintained a sizeable manufacturing base. Manufacturing represents almost a third of the Korean economy, for example, and only a tenth of ours.

As we emerge from this crisis, our priority must be to reindustrialise our economy, making it more resilient and creating better-quality, more-secure jobs for workers. The government should prioritise a strategy for industrial renaissance and national resilience that looks to create manufacturing hubs by providing direct government seed-funding and incentives for manufacturing firms to invest in the UK. We should have a revolution in vocational education involving businesses and unions. We should introduce centres of advanced manufacturing excellence in partnership with major employers. And we should look to re-shore jobs that had previously been offshored.

Reindustrialisation should be a priority for economic, social and national security reasons. Manufacturing jobs tend to boost productivity more than from other sectors and contribute more to the kind of innovation that successful economies need. Such an effort to put the UK at the global forefront of manufacturing will not be easy but will make the economy much more resilient in the event of future crises and major shocks. We'll also restore economic pride to many communities and restore dignity to work. The UK must ensure that the Covid crisis means that the long-promised move towards a different type of economy actually becomes a reality.

EMMA GRIFFIN

RETHINKING WORK

Perhaps no aspect of our lives has come into such sharp focus in recent months as the meaning of work. At times like this, my hero Bertrand Russell is always worth turning to. His essay 'In Praise of Idleness' (1932) contains the following, irresistible quote: 'First of all, what is work? Work is of two kinds: first, altering the position of matter at or near the earth's surface relatively to other such matter; second, telling other people to do so. The first kind is unpleasant and ill paid; the second is pleasant and highly paid.' When my dad first read these words to me, an epoch ago, I remember thinking that Russell ought to have added the first kind is generally done by women, and the second men.

As the historian Emma Griffin notes, women's work has been much more seriously affected than men's by this pandemic. Both in terms of the paid kind that shows up in employment figures, and the unpaid, domestic and emotional kind that goes unrecognised but is just as, if not more, important. Domestic labour – whose utter drudgery and necessity are in proportion – remains mostly the province of women. These patterns within couples are often reinforced by parenthood and have been exacerbated by the pandemic. Many of the injustices that earlier generations of feminists fought don't just remain with us. They're getting worse.

Covid-19 has brought to the fore the universal division around which all known societies have been structured: that between men and women. As a medical phenomenon, it is clear that Covid-19 affects men far more seriously than women, with the male death rate twice that of the female – a difference that can't be explained away by reference to lifestyle.

Yet as a social event, Covid disproportionately disadvantages women. Because women are more likely to work part-time and on zero-hours contracts, and because of the sectors they work in, they have been more likely to have lost work – thereby increasing the already dismal income gap between the sexes. And regardless of whether or not they work, women have picked up a greater share of the childcare and home-schooling responsibilities that lockdown has imposed.

It is also perhaps worth reminding ourselves that crises don't always have the effect of imposing conservative social norms. If we look back at upheavals such as the First or Second World Wars, the immediate impact was to increase women's participation in the labour market and to enhance their income, though these gains admittedly often proved short-lived. Yet this time, we don't even have grounds for a little hope or optimism, as we appear to be defaulting into centuries-old patterns, whereby the home, and everything in it, is a woman's business.

This is not to deny that great progress has been made over the past 50 years – legislation around equal pay and maternity rights, childcare and after-school clubs have immensely helped women to forge independent lives outside the home. The more difficult problem remains sorting out the housework. Modern conveniences reduce the domestic burden, but they don't eliminate it and there's no way to automate the raising of children. And what government is going to legislate for who washes the dishes and who puts the kids to bed?

Perhaps this is the moment for us to reorient our understandings of the meaning of work and of its place in our lives. Running a home is also work – and if you're not doing it, then somebody else is doing it for you. Recent research calculates that the unpaid work young women do for their families is worth an astonishing £140 billion a year to the UK economy – that's more than is generated by our entire financial sector. It's time to challenge our rigid adherence to the view that only paid work really counts. And while our politicians cannot control what goes on in our homes, they certainly can play a role in deciding what counts, what can be measured and what needs to change.

CALEB FEMI

RETHINKING EDUCATION

When he was 17, the poet and director Caleb Femi, who grew up in Peckham, south London, had a gun put to his head. The trigger was pulled. It's only because the gun jammed that you can read him here.

Femi's essay puts me in mind of another important thinker in this arena. In his book Culture Counts, *the late Sir Roger Scruton wrote: 'It is one of the most deeply rooted superstitions of our age that the purpose of education is to benefit those who receive it.' He went on: 'True teachers do not provide Knowledge as a benefit to their pupils. They treat their pupils as a benefit to Knowledge.' For Scruton, knowledge, and not the pupil, is the supreme consideration. Femi has a similar motive in arguing for a new kind of learning, while – like Scruton – endorsing the noble idea that education has a value beyond utility: that is, beyond maximising economic potential.*

Femi forces us to ask, as Roger Scruton asked: why do we educate? For decades now, we have pushed ever greater numbers of pupils towards university, redefining aspects of university in the process. Perhaps, as Femi suggests, optimising the moral – as opposed to material – value of education requires us to reassess our grade expectations.

The British education system has covered itself in a veil for centuries. The veil is the promise that at the end of the road of education, there is security and even prosperity.

We are told to trim the fat of our potential – to focus simply on gaining academic qualifications to the detriment of our other talents or interests. Students turned up every morning for 39 weeks a year. They studied and they learned for tests and they sat those tests.

This system shrank their imagination and the autonomy of the learning process, but there was that promise that you would leave with a qualification, an emblem that said you were a capable member of society. This was the veil.

Covid-19 was the storm that tore that veil apart for most students in the UK. When the lockdown was imposed, schools had to close and students taking A-levels and GCSEs, as well as some from Years 9 and 10 in the middle of exam prep, were told that they wouldn't be able to take their tests.

Imagine that, after years of classroom exercises, homework, coursework, mock tests, parents' evenings and sacrificing so much because of that promise of a qualification, of security.

Instead, your worth, the value of your qualification, your supposed future prospects would be based on a calculation of what is called your predicted grade. Take note that statistically, black students are under-predicted and generally exceed their predicted grade in their real exams.

So what many students learned during this lockdown period is that society is an uncertain landscape, and job sectors are volatile. And then they began to question themselves. They questioned the tools that they have to be able to survive in the wild that is adulthood.

You don't have to be David Attenborough to know that the absolute that is security does not exist in nature. The ones who survive, the ones who thrive, are the ones who have the tools and the skills to adapt.

So, as a student you have to question yourself – do I have the tools that are required to survive in this society? These tools are problem-solving, creativity, innovation, the autonomy to envisage a new possibility and a new future. Also, the mental dexterity to make careers for yourself and make society a more efficient place, a more equal place for everyone. These tools that you need to have to survive in such an uncertain landscape don't match up with the ones you learned at school.

Going forward, it means that it's ultimately a job for you, the individual, alongside the community, to think in ways that put you in the driving seat of your own learning.

New approaches need to be made where students are encouraged to think creatively, to exercise their imagination, to problem-solve in unique, innovative, exciting ways. That is what a post-lockdown relationship with education should look like.

GINA MCCARTHY

RETHINKING ACTIVISM

For decades, Gina McCarthy has been cited by campaigners around the world as an inspiration: someone who got things done, rather than merely talking about them. Presidents Obama and Biden both gave her big jobs. This essay was written while she was at the helm of the Natural Resources Defense Council, but public health and the environment have been the focus of her entire career..

McCarthy notes that when she started her career, dreadful pollution was a common part of life in big cities, but today citizens expect better. That didn't happen by accident: it was the result of patient, passionate campaigning. At the core of her essay is the explicit linking of today's social media-driven activism with Earth Day, a monumental institution in the history of environmentalism and protesting, which celebrated its 50th birthday in 2020. The function of activism, as McCarthy relates it, is to shift public consciousness and mobilise leadership, but as a prelude only to the acquisition of legislative power. That, in her telling, is how you get things done. Though you need the activist energy first.

To my mind, the lesson of her career, and her essay, is that if big change is what you're after, it's better to be inside the tent than outside.

Growing up in Boston, I could see, taste and feel pollution all around me. My third-grade classmates and I used to run to shut the windows at my school when the stench from the rubber company next door started to waft in. And it wasn't until years later that I figured out just how many people in and around that plant had died from brain cancer, one of them a dear friend of mine. I can't help but wonder if her classmates had just been a little bit slower than mine at shutting the windows. You know, I started a career in public health and the environment because I wanted something better for myself and for my children.

And we've come so far since then. Gone is the black smoke spewing out of smokestacks. Today, if you go swimming in Boston Harbor, you're not likely to have to peel tar balls off your legs, like my family and I did back in the day. Why? Because 50 years ago, 20 million people got together for the first Earth Day and they said, 'Enough's enough.' They stirred a movement that resulted in real and lasting change. And guess what? It's happening again today. Young activists, women leaders, people of color, old dudes like me are commanding the attention of local and global leaders on issues from climate change to racial justice. And when I look at the faces of my two beautiful grandchildren, I'm not going to be sitting on the sidelines. I have no intention of letting them down.

They're just getting started in a world that's in crisis. Racial violence against black Americans, an unprecedented pandemic and climate change, all at the same time. It would be easy to say the challenges are too big to solve. But we can solve them, and we must. And we will. We will build a more just and equitable world. We can and we must rebuild from this pandemic by investing in a healthier, more sustainable and more just future. A future that will empower people and drive prosperity. That means finally saying goodbye to fossil fuels and embracing the clean energy solutions that are at our fingertips. So, let's go all in and let's invest in it. A clean, healthy, just and sustainable future is all about lower energy bills and millions of new good-paying jobs, where workers are valued and protected. It's a world where no community is left behind, a world full of hope and opportunity. It is a world that is absolutely possible and necessary for us to build together. We just have to demand it. So, let me ask you one question. What are we all waiting for?

TARA WESTOVER

RETHINKING THE EDUCATION DIVIDE

By common consent, Tara Westover's Educated *was one of the most riveting memoirs of our time. In it, she described the suffocation and frustration of growing up in a family of radical Mormon survivalists – and the liberation and exhilaration that the pursuit of knowledge gave her. As Westover cogently argues, post-war societies across the world have venerated cognitive skill as a gold standard in human endeavour, and the route to success in the 'achievement society'. There are noble grounds for doing this: a society that upholds knowledge rather than, say, brute force, is likely to be more civilised.*

But there has been a cost to this, which illuminates the deficiencies of meritocracy – namely, that those who don't have a great education, and thereby don't achieve lofty status, can feel a sense of indignity or shame. No wonder, as Westover notes, education – perhaps even more than wealth – is today one of the great dividing lines within the West, a reliable indicator of both voting intention and life chances. Amid a technological revolution that is making access to learning much more widespread, reimagining what education is for, and reinserting the development of character as an integral part of it, is a pressing social challenge.

In the early days of this pandemic, we were told that Covid-19 would be the 'great equaliser' – that it would bring us together because it would affect everyone alike. Rich and poor, urban and rural, members of every racial group. Those with advanced degrees, and those who never finished primary school.

The idea was that a germ is not subject to those prejudices to which human beings so often are. It is not impressed by money or dazzled by prestige. It does not see skin colour, or subscribe to stereotypes of gender. A germ is blind biology. Its one virtue was its supposed lack of prejudice.

Of course, none of that turned out to be true.

The virus was not blind. It devastated men more than women; the old more than the young; and in America, where I live, and in many other places, racial minorities suffered disproportionately.

So did the poor. So did the less educated. The virus, it turned out, was deeply prejudiced.

But there was one meaningful way that it was, in fact, a kind of equaliser, and that was that it made us remember the many forgotten people whose hard work make our lives possible.

I noticed the change about a week into the crisis. A friend of mine ordered an online delivery, and he added a 50 per cent tip. 'Anyone out delivering curry in a pandemic,' he said, 'has earned every penny.' A week later, a pipe burst in the house I was staying in. I was suddenly without running water. But the next morning, a man came, wearing a fabric mask. He replaced the pipe, and I had water.

He did not have the luxury of sitting at home in a quarantine. He had chosen to risk it – to help me, to protect his livelihood. And the same choice is made every day by nurses and cooks and cashiers and truckers and factory workers.

For all the difficult stories that have come out of this, perhaps the most moving is that nightly racket made on the streets of New York and other cities as people holler and whistle and bang pans to thank frontline workers. Doctors and nurses, yes, but also caretakers and delivery people, grocers and electricians. A whole army of people who leave their homes every day to keep the rest of us safe and well. These are not the rich and illustrious. They are not the so-called elite. They are often not paid very well for what they do. Many of them did not go to college, and for that reason they are sometimes looked down on by those who did have that privilege.

I've been thinking lately that education has become the new social divider, perhaps even more than wealth. We forget that in many cases, wealth and education go together. That education has itself become a privilege reserved for those who can pay for it. Our modern economy has a great hunger for college-educated workers, and the result was that many of our workers all over the world felt dismissed and left behind. They felt there was no place for them in the world we are making.

We have, I think, become a little prejudiced against work. We seem to believe that if someone is not credentialled, they must not be industrious. We tacitly accepted the idea that the professional classes are somehow harder working or more deserving of respect than the people who work with their hands. But everyone deserves respect. And more than respect; they deserve to be paid. They deserve the kind of pay that will allow them to live a dignified life. My friend Jia Tolentino recently observed in the *New Yorker* that there is something corrupt about a system in which essential workers are paid so little that they cannot survive the emergencies through which they sustain the rest of us.

So here's what I hope we remember as we set about to rebuild our post-coronavirus world. I hope we remember the people who keep the lights on and the factories open, the farms stocked and the pipes clear. Who cook, farm, drive, caretake, plumb, wire, wash and build.

I hope we remember that we are not two peoples – not the elite and the non-elite, the college-educated and not, the urban and rural, the white collar and the blue. We are one people. Let's build a world in which we can be one people.

KWAME ANTHONY APPIAH

RETHINKING THE POWER OF SMALL ACTIONS

In his 1973 seminal short work Small Is Beautiful, *E.F. Schu-macher argued for economics as if people mattered. A focus on big corporations and macroeconomics had, he claimed, left people behind. Better to talk about economics in relatable terms: at the local, neighbourhood level. The philosopher and novelist Kwame Anthony Appiah applies this argument to the urgent moral questions of our time.*

A seeming paradox of all moral crises is that because they depend so much on collective action, individuals often feel they lack agency. If I violate some social norm, by litter-ing in the park, say, or refusing to vote, perhaps it will go unnoticed. This seductive idea is wrong and counterproduc-tive. As Appiah cogently puts it, collective action is but the sum of individual actions.

As an undergraduate obsessed with philosophy, I came across the Australian utilitarian Peter Singer, who happens to be the founder of a website Appiah cites. It had a profound

*effect on me. Small acts can have extraordinary moral conse-
quences, for the betterment of people near or far. In recent
years, huge advances in social psychology have shown the
deep power of social norms to influence us: we take our cues
from those around us. If Appiah and Singer can, between
them, make us – make you – rethink your moral agency, the
post-pandemic world could yet be a better place.*

In 2020, the iconic accessory of the coronavirus
pandemic was a face mask. Reading its moral meaning required recognising that we wore them not so much
to protect ourselves as to save others. Because many
who spread the virus have no symptoms, we couldn't
easily know whether we were infectious. And so we
wore the masks.

One or two unmasked people won't make much
difference, of course. But one or two failures to pay your
fare on the underground won't bankrupt the system
either, and that doesn't make jumping the turnstile okay.
Morality requires us to do our part in collective practices
that are good for the community, even when our single
violation poses little threat. What's important is that we
can pull off something wonderful if we all stick to the
rule – we can contain the spread of a virus that can be
devastating, even lethal, for so many. And, *if* we pull this
off, we will have done so together, at the cost of some
inconvenience to each of us.

The larger shutdown, of course, has had enormous effects, locally and globally, in terms of lost livelihoods and more. But masks themselves – which have been key to re-entry, an easing of restrictions, from Korea to Germany – have never demanded very much from us. They represent a small levy that can end up raising a vast sum.

In this way, the mask is symbolic of the solutions to other problems the human community must face together. Climate change is still accelerating; there are nearly 80 million refugees in the world today as the year 2020 comes to an end; global poverty blights the prospects of billions. Each of these problems is open to solutions that are like wearing a mask: we can master them if we make wise plans and everyone plays their small part in carrying them out. Even if a single failure to do so may not do much harm, it's wrong not to do your part. And if each of us *does* do our part, we can do something great together.

Voting is another example of a collective act in which each of us plays a small but crucial part: when you vote, you're participating in a collective action that can reshape your society. It took more than 80 million American votes to elect Joe Biden. The same goes for measures that could have a significant impact on the environment. In America, where I live, the National Resources Defense Council, an environmental group, says that if we Americans kept our tyres properly inflated, we could save 1.2 billion gallons of petrol each year. That costs you only the time of a regular check-up when you're buying petrol. The Life You Can Save is an online website whose collective donations are literally saving lives among the global poor. In 2020, they had a special campaign for Covid-19 relief. A world-changing measure of development assistance would result if the reasonably well-off people gave a small fraction of their earnings. For someone earning £50,000 a year, we're talking about the cost of a latte every couple of days.

It would take time for a campaign to turn practices like these into norms to which we're all committed. But it's surely time worth spending. And, since, unlike a face mask, a properly inflated tyre or a charitable gift is not visible at a glance, you'll need to discuss it with friends and family and, maybe, sport a bumper sticker or two: have you checked your tyre pressure lately? Have you given to save lives? Are you voting? To entrench these norms, we need to spread this simple message: that if each of us does our small part, we can change the world for the better.

CHARLOTTE LYDIA RILEY

RETHINKING UNIVERSITIES

What are universities for? In The Idea of a University, *published in 1854, Cardinal John Henry Newman described it as 'a place of concourse, whither students come from every quarter for every kind of knowledge. You cannot have the best of every kind everywhere; you must go to some great city or emporium for it.' Nothing about this romantic, even noble, vision of higher education stipulates that you must be 18. So why do we treat university as mainly a rite of passage for the young?*

Lockdown has been tough for those involved in university life. For students, it has led to deep frustration, deferred years, unsat exams, and even golden summers lost. For academics and administrators in this vastly expanded sector, there are huge financial worries. Yet for some of those involved, this has also been a rare opportunity for inclusion, as the historian Dr Charlotte Lydia Riley argues. Might we now reinvent university as something you dip in and out of throughout life?

If university is a place of possibility, as Riley argues, why not keep those possibilities going throughout our lives? Those of us who are fortunate enough to have gone to university often wonder what we would have done differently in retrospect. If 'lifelong learning' really meant something, perhaps we could give ourselves a second chance.

My final-year students in summer 2020 are graduating into a world that is different to when they arrived at university. Some of my colleagues graduated just as the Berlin Wall fell, or at the end of apartheid, or into a post-9/11 world; I finished my master's in the midst of the 2008 financial crash. Every generation has their story, their big historical event. Our finalists packed up their student flats hastily in March; they finished their dissertations in childhood bedrooms and handed them in by email; they'll have their graduation parties on a video-call.

Covid-19 has been a challenge for universities – lectures online, seminars with cats and toddlers in the background, no libraries, no offices, no campus. But it's also a moment to think about what is valuable. For some people it's been a rare chance of inclusion, in a system that often excludes them. People with disabilities, people with full-time jobs or caring responsibilities, people who can't afford fees or don't normally feel welcome on campus or wouldn't ever think of coming to a public lecture; who don't want to be seen to have pretensions, or worry they wouldn't understand. In the last three months these people might actually have been able to dial in and listen to a talk, while doing the washing up, or propped up in bed, or rocking a baby. How can we preserve that wonderful thing, and take it further?

I have more questions than answers right now. But I've been thinking a lot about universities as spaces of possibility.

In normal times, you walk into a lecture theatre full of freshers on the first day of term and you see all these faces, looking down at you. And it's a moment where the possibilities stretch out like the future – the weeks until the end of term, the terms that make up the year, the years of the degree. Many of our students – not all of them, but many of them – arrive just on the cusp of adulthood and discover who they are while they are studying history, or maths, or media studies, or medicine. And some of them are older, and they're with us because they've made a new decision about themselves and their lives. For all of them, they exist in that moment with the rare capacity for possibility.

And if education is a space of possibility above all else, what can we do to preserve that? If we want education to be a possibility for everyone – if we hold open university education for everyone who wants it – what changes do we need to embrace?

We need to make it possible for students to join us when they are ready, to keep a seat for them, and make a space where they will feel welcome and safe. Lifelong learning should mean just that – it should mean both that university education is part of a longer process, and also that your final exams, whenever they are, don't mean the end of learning. Not just useful practical information, but also education for the sake of it. And it should also mean that people can access formal education at any point in their life when it makes the most sense for them. University isn't right for everyone at 18, but it might be when they're 28, or 38, or 68.

At the moment, university communities are disrupted and fractured. We are scattered across the world trying to keep track of one other. After all this is over, we will want to get back to normal – to restore our communities. But maybe it's also a chance to throw open our doors and to welcome more people in, to a world of possibility.

K.K. SHAILAJA

RETHINKING DEVELOPMENT

*K.K. Shailaja, better known as Shailaja Teacher, is the revered
minister of health and social welfare of Kerala State.*

*Kerala in south India has long rivalled Scandinavia and
the Baltics as the place to glean lessons on developing human
capital. Run by a communist party, it has an exceptional
record on literacy and numeracy, and also a very impressive
record in public health, as you'll hear. That is partly because
of the hugely constructive and indeed apolitical role science
plays in Keralan government. And this essay is nothing if not
an invitation to ask precisely what the power of science in our
lives can be. In Britain, politicians have leaned heavily on
scientific advice, even injecting a fraudulent definite article
into the phrase 'the science says', as if every scientist around the
world concurs. In Shailaja's reckoning, science is not merely an
instrument of progress and therefore development. It can also
save us from ourselves.*

*My father is from the state next to Kerala, Tamil Nadu.
When Shailaja says she wants to 'convert the conservative*

societies to develop scientific thinking', I know exactly what she means. She isn't talking about societies that vote Conservative with a big C. She's talking about cultures that have deeply ingrained habits, rituals and superstitions, which happen to include a resistance to embracing modern medicine.

A strong public health system and accessibility for poor people to get treatment from it – that is the most important thing. Money or financing alone will not help us. We need planning that is people-centred. Each and every person, the whole population, should get accessible treatment and also affordable treatment. That should be the slogan throughout the world. Only then can we resist this kind of infectious disease. Every challenge gives us some opportunities. Most of us understand that we should fight together, united, against this killer virus. This gives us some opportunities too. For example, everyone is now discussing people-centred planning and also the basic systems, basic structures, etc.

In Kerala, we have done well in some health indices; we are at the forefront. Our child mortality rate is seven out of 1,000. In some countries, this is about 20 or 40. Kerala has achieved a very good result in that. When the UN declared their sustainable development goals (SDGs), we also declared some SDGs here. One element was to reduce the child mortality rate, another was to reduce the maternal mortality rate. And we tried our best. Now, at this time, when we are facing this challenge of the corona-virus and thousands of human beings are dying, we must learn the lesson that we should invest more money in the primary health system or the public health system. The other thing is that if we can save people from this virus, there is an opportunity to increase investment in the industrial sectors, for example, by helping small-scale industries start up. Kerala is now trying for that.

Now, in Kerala, we are using modern technology to trace the positive cases and the contacts. We are using IT and that is another opportunity. We tend to think about this sort of thing only if we are facing a challenge. That is the inclination of the world. But I think the whole world is now thinking about science too. Only science can save us, nothing else. That is the most positive thing. Now people are thinking about science; they are eagerly look-ing to see whether scientists are discovering a vaccine or finding out anything that could save human beings. And that is an opportunity to make this world scientific. It is a chance to convert the conservative societies, to develop scientific thinking and to promote scientific culture.

SAMANTHA POWER

RETHINKING GLOBAL GOVERNANCE

In her memoir, The Education of an Idealist, *Samantha Power, former US Ambassador to the UN and Professor of Practice at Harvard Law School and Harvard Kennedy School, confronts one of the central paradoxes of our time. The most pressing challenges today require international cooperation. But many elements of international cooperation, already under strain before Covid-19, are buckling.*

Many of the recommendations Power makes are familiar. But they gain authority and urgency not only from her career at the top of international diplomacy, but from the fact that the basic rights she wants to see become universal seem to be under threat.

I detect a dark undertone to this essay. Power seems to be saying that, for all the possibilities Covid-19 affords us, there are underlying trends that do not bode well. I was also struck by her strong emphasis on healthy institutions, which reflect the best and worst of the countries from whence they spring. After the

massacre that ended in 1945, the world invented new institu-
tions to address the greatest challenges of that era. Do we need to
do the same today? And if so, might Samantha Power, a deter-
mined diplomat and idealist, play an important role in them?

Although public health experts have been warning for years that the world was unprepared for a large-scale pandemic, few might have predicted one aspect of the response – the show of individual and collective solidarity that, in the early months of the pandemic, shut down entire nations. Even though the United States, for example, was led in 2020 by a president who encouraged anti-science and anti-lockdown views, most Americans still answered the call to comply with highly restrictive health guidelines – despite knowing that doing so would cause severe economic pain. In just months the result of this collective sacrifice globally, according to the UN, was the loss of some 305 million jobs world-wide, but the prevention of hundreds of millions of new coronavirus infections and the avoidance of more than 3 million Covid-related deaths in Europe alone. Remarkably, people taking preventive steps reported themselves more motivated by the desire to protect others than to protect themselves.

So, what can we glean from this? Of course, as a general rule, we can agree that people don't want to get sick and die. But more profoundly, we can largely recognise that no man is an island and, by and large, that we want to help and not harm others – even if this requires making some sacrifices ourselves. As the temptation beckons to ease up on social distancing, we must recommit ourselves to these truths while the pandemic still rages. And when the worst of the pandemic is behind us, we must do the same in creating a revamped and much more far-sighted international system. Given severe, ongoing tensions between the US and China, this won't be easy. The lure of zero-sum thinking in Washington and Beijing is strong. But if anything reminds us of the futility of a go-it-alone mindset, it is the devastation caused by a pandemic that respects no borders.

The elements of a reformed global system would be, first and foremost, dramatic improvements in national governance. Simply put, an inter-governmental system can't function if the governments comprising that system do not competently govern. The late US diplomat Richard Holbrooke once remarked that blaming the United Nations for a crisis was like blaming Madison Square Garden when the New York Knicks play badly: you are blaming a building. International institutions gather the best and worst habits and practices of the nation states that comprise them; Covid-19 will not change that. But the institutional weaknesses that the pandemic exposed inside countries, and the growing hunger for reality-based leadership among voters, provides an opening for significant domestic reforms, in which far greater emphasis is placed on confronting economic inequality and racial injustice, replacing decaying infrastructure and bridging partisan divides.

Second, global cooperative bodies, currently comprised of governments, should both incorporate and be supplemented by much more diverse networks that rely not only on states for funding and expertise but also on nongovernmental organisations, foundations, private sector innovators and mobilised citizens who now, more readily, see their fates as tied to the improved performance of broad-based international coalitions.

Third and finally, the world's open societies must recognise that basic freedoms are coming under severe threat. Chinese President Xi Jinping and other autocrats would like nothing more than to rewrite the rules of the international system, aligning them more closely with their preference that international bodies become far more deferential to state power. They want these bodies to undertake less human rights promotion and enforcement, be less transparent, and offer less independent monitoring, at just the time when the world needs much more of each. Countries dedicated to science, pluralism and democratic values therefore need to stand together within global fora, on behalf of our common humanity and common security.

RETHINKING THE MUSIC INDUSTRY

Who owns art? Who owns culture of any kind? Is it the artist?
Is it the state, which might tax creativity to achieve greater
welfare? Or perhaps it's the audience, who in the moment
of appreciation – looking at a portrait, say, or listening
to some magnificent tune – achieve that moment of tran-
scendent connection or ecstasy which saints and poets have
forever described.

Almost certainly nobody ever thought an ideal answer to
the above questions would be 'just three companies'. Yet just
three companies own 70 per cent of all music, ever. As with
so many aspects of the internet, the gains for consumers in
convenience come with costs that seem invisible – even though
they're anything but.

In my own profession, journalism, the past decade has been
a grim procession of collapsing business models and incessant
redundancies, as the internet made general news a universally
available commodity, expected for free. Yet in recent years,
there has been a revival of the idea that quality costs; that

there is no shame in asking consumers of digital content to pay; and that creating a direct relationship with them, rather than going through a few platforms owned by billionaires on distant shores, is vital. A similar principle is the best hope for musicians too. Otherwise, even when live music returns, many face immiseration.

There's no getting around it; Covid-19 has been disastrous for music.

Live performance has disappeared, with no real return in sight, and venues that license music to play in public have been closed for months. The only remaining, reliable source of income for artists is streaming.

Music listening has been made wonderfully convenient by streaming and our opportunities for music discovery have never been greater. But it was never built for this stress test because it was never built to sustain and foster the music economy. Bluntly, it pays artists and songwriters very, very badly.

The economics of streaming have been structured to do two things: to make music as cheap as possible – often free – so that tech firms can enjoy take up of their technologies, and to reward the major rights-holders, i.e. the major record labels.

It's a bewildering fact that three music companies now have ownership of over 70 per cent of all the recorded music made in the history of the world. The deals they leveraged with tech firms are the grounds on which artists are so particularly failed.

Every streaming user's money is thrown into one big pot. It's then divided among the record labels based on the total consumption of their catalogues. This forms a paradox: if the amount of music keeps going up, and it will, and the number of users plateaus, as it inevitably does, the value of an individual piece of music, in this system, will always go down. Spotify is presently paying less than a third of a penny per play and this figure has dropped nearly every year since their inception. If you're a major label, owning nearly all the music and continuing to acquire more from which to earn your billions, this hardly matters, but if you are an artist that's your work being consistently devalued.

Clearly creators need to get a bigger share of streaming revenues ... but there's something else to address. As of now, your money doesn't go to the music you listen to. For an average user, less than two quid of your tenner might go to the individuals you listen to. Instead, your money goes to music that is being played continuously in the background somewhere else. But your money can go to your music.

This is something called the User-Centric Payment System. Instead of your money heading to that big indiscriminate pot, it goes to exactly what you're listening to. Besides giving the consumer a direct relationship with their favourite artists and moral rights, this has many other benefits. Niche music, regional tastes, classical and jazz all start to see money; more money stays in regional and national economies; smaller artists finally have a chance at funding, and, with each new user, more money goes to the music they're choosing to listen to.

That's why I'm supporting the #BrokenRecord campaign. The economics and the culture of streaming needs to change, and put music makers and, significantly, music lovers at its heart.

REBECCA ADLINGTON

RETHINKING THE ATHLETE'S LIFE

Most people, when they look back on their life, say the thing they treasure most, and wish they had more of, is time with loved ones. Despite all the anguish that has attended lockdown, it has forced parents to spend more time with their children. Even if they are former Olympic gold medallists with obsessive fitness regimes, like Rebecca Adlington.

In this wonderfully upbeat essay, Adlington, who has a five-year-old daughter, provides riveting insight. Not into parenthood; rather, into what being an Olympian actually involves. Short answer: it's hell. The gruelling training regimes, the early morning starts and non-negotiable diets, the endless corporate obligations and media requests … there just aren't enough hours in the day to nurture the precious bonds closer to home. The only solution, according to Adlington, is to – to coin a phrase – take back control.

All of us can relate to the idea that the time we have with loved ones is precious, and something we won't get back. And her advice to athletes, to let go of all distractions from things you just can't control, sounds like the kind of unarguable common sense that businesses, politicians and leaders across society ought to learn from. Huge thanks to this remarkable competitor for a wise reminder of what we should know already.

Lockdown has changed all of our lives. It's certainly changed mine significantly. The quality time I've been able to spend with my five-year-old daughter is something I wouldn't normally have had. I certainly never had an opportunity like this with my family or my parents growing up. We've had time to bond and build on our relationship in a deeper, better way and she's grown up so much from having the one-to-one attention. She's developed skills and enjoyed tasks that we wouldn't have normally had the opportunity to do when she is at school.

So, she's done things like learning how to ride a bike, and helping and learning around the house, as well as exercising with me. Normally I work out or do jobs around the house when she's at school, but now we do them together which is really nice, and I hope I've been a good example to her and helped her develop that lifestyle, especially as she gets older. We've had time to just stop and just be with each other more. No more running from place to place; it's just been about sitting, talking, laughing, playing and snuggling together. And I'm definitely more aware of this coming out of lockdown and making sure to include it in our day-to-day life.

We all forget to slow down at times. And one thing I have thought about during lockdown was how I would have dealt with that time if I was still competing as an elite athlete. As an elite athlete your schedule is mapped out for you. You know when competitions are, when you're training, when you have a little bit of time off. Normally you're up at 5am, you're training, you're doing gym work, you've got physio, massage, sports psychology, sponsor and team commitments, as well as just time to eat and recover. You have to fill in where you're going to be 24/7 for drug testing, as well as trying obviously to see friends and family, but you have to be selfish and you have to focus on performance 24/7.

Even on Sundays when you're having a day off, you have to be aware of how that day will impact your performance or the training for the week ahead. The lockdown period has been a completely new experience for every single athlete. A chance to reflect, to slow down, to take the pressure off. Sport is such a high-pressured, intense environment every single day, and lockdown has been a time to try new things and different activities, remembering why you got into sport in the first place without the focus on competition.

That's why my lesson to learn from lockdown is how important it is to focus on what you can control. Just enjoy the process, enjoy the journey. It's not just about that outcome or your next competition. That competition, obviously, is important. As it motivates us, it excites us, it also comes with pressure and expectations. If it were me during that time of lockdown, I would have actually really enjoyed trying new ways to stay fit. Even though I think I would have lost the feel for the water, I think you can get that back within a few weeks or months. Certainly you can make up that time, especially with a year to go until the next Olympics.

I think for me it would have been mentally a lot, lot tougher. As an athlete you stick to a four-year cycle and everything is dedicated to that time, but now we have a full year longer. Everything you built up for, to peak at that exact right time and that particular time – all of a sudden that goal has moved. It's difficult maintaining that level and keeping that momentum going, but lockdown has affected the whole world. We have all been in this together.

The sporting community I don't think has probably felt much stronger than it has right now, as everyone is in the same boat. Physically you can only have done so much during this time, so the mental aspect is huge. I've no doubt that everyone is itching to get back into training, even competing, seeing their teammates and their squad mates, and this time has probably made athletes even more driven to succeed. The younger athletes have had an opportunity to bridge the gap. They've had extra time to develop and grow. Other athletes, who might have been struggling or injured, will have just seized this opportunity. It's been a gift of time for them.

I hope when we are all fully out of lockdown that athletes will remember to focus on what they can control. We can't control when venues will open, when we'll be able to travel again properly, what effects the restrictions will have, or what even the future of sport will look like. But we can focus on what we can control and how we are using this time and how we will have been able to develop and adapt moving forward.

And I don't think this is just about athletes; it's a lesson for everyone. We all need to focus on what we can control at this time and all I can do is look after my daughter, make the most of our time together, as it's time I will never ever get back, and I will have memories that I will cherish forever.

Brenda Hale

RETHINKING HOW WE DO TRIALS

What does it mean, during a pandemic, to get a 'fair hearing'? With her calm demeanour, decades of experience and erudition, Lady Hale has much to contribute to any conversation about reforming the law of the land.

To outsiders – many of whom want to remain outsiders – the legal system as represented by the courts is a forbidding, even scary place. Its strange rituals and dress, frequently grand architecture, unapologetic jargon and clear hierarchies all enforce the distinction between upholders of the law and those who violate it. Yet in this magisterial defence of those traditions, Lady Hale makes the case for courts that convene physically rather than virtually, while also making the case for gentle reform.

Perhaps you too will detect just a hint of irony in her reference to 'sombre clothing'. This from the baroness whose spider-shaped brooch not only went viral in September 2019, when she ruled that a British prime minister had acted unlawfully, but also led to countless columns and newspaper inches in search of its true meaning. Lady Hale's specific recommendations about reform of trials deserve at least as much attention.

Lockdown has forced the courts to find ways to ensure that urgent cases can still be heard, some of them pretty makeshift. But it has also taught us some valuable lessons about what is and is not important to a fair hearing: one which not only produces the right result but is felt to be fair, by the judges and the lawyers, and by the people whose cases these are. This gives us the opportunity to rethink how we do trials, in all kinds of cases. We do have some sacred cows: our reliance on oral hearings, oral evidence, oral argument, and in many cases oral decisions; our belief that a witness's demeanour and body language can reveal whether he or she is telling the truth; and perhaps above all, our faith in trial by a jury of 12 randomly selected members of the public as the greatest protection against the wrongful conviction of the innocent.

Routine case management decisions can and should be taken in writing or remotely, as can uncontested matters, such as debt collection, divorce decrees and guilty pleas. But anything contested is a different matter. As Celia Kitzinger says, there is a gravitas attached to a courtroom hearing: the formal architecture and courtroom layout; the elevated and distant seat of the judge; the familiar rituals; and the sombre clothing. All are evidence of the seriousness and impartiality with which decisions are taken. All are lost if everyone is appearing remotely on small screens from their own homes or offices or, worse still, invisibly over the phone. That feels more like a case conference than a judicial process. Also, as an unnamed family court judge says, he or she is deprived of all the usual ways of creating an atmosphere of trust, fairness and compassion: reassuring smiles; listening intently to what the parties are saying; assessing their level of anxiety and nerves. It is all too easy for the professionals to forget that the lay parties are there and listening if they cannot be seen – they should never have to do so alone and unsupported. Trials should not be experienced as a conspiracy of the lawyers against the laity.

Some of these problems could be cured by providing much more sophisticated platforms for remote hearings, but not all. There is nothing quite like the gathering at court to encourage negotiation and agreement. And what about the face-to-face encounter when witnesses give their evidence? Children and vulnerable witnesses can already give their evidence by video link. Some think that this is not as powerful as giving it in the courtroom – it looks like television rather than reality. But there could be advantages in separating the witness and the cross-examiner: less intimidating and confusing, especially where violence is alleged. Should we invest in more and better video-links or in larger courtrooms?

And what about face coverings? We are reluctant to allow Muslim women to give evidence wearing the niqab – the face veil. I found it easy to tell whether a mother was telling the truth once she had taken off her veil. But could we allow or require witnesses to wear the non-surgical masks which everyone now has to wear in various public settings?

And might face masks be the answer to jury trials? A good jury turns into a little community, working together in the interests of justice. This is lost if they are operating remotely or even at a social distance in a courtroom. But a more radical solution would be to rethink why and when we need a jury trial. Should we reduce the number of cases where there is a right to choose trial by jury? Should we reduce the number of jurors, perhaps to seven (as in inquests)? Should we replace some jury trials by trial by judge alone? A judge has to give detailed reasons for his decision, whereas juries do not. But judges can get case hardened. Better still might be a judge sitting with two lay people – rather like the jurat system in the Channel Islands.

We do have a golden opportunity for a radical rethink of how we do trials. Let's hope that it is taken.

Nisha Katona

RETHINKING
HOSPITALITY

For nearly six years I was a restaurant critic. I must have eaten out at hundreds of restaurants across the UK and have been overweight all my life. (First world problems, I know.) I am fascinated by the history of different global cuisines, and an occasional judge on Masterchef. So when Katona – who spent 20 years as a barrister before quitting to follow her passion – made this case for our benighted, battered restaurant trade, my heart-strings were well and truly plucked.

Covid-19 has wrought devastation on tens of thousands of establishments, full of very industrious people who work anti-social hours, usually for love of food rather than money. All have tried to adapt to an ever more digital world. But it turns out there's more to restaurants than mere grub on a plate. It's almost enough to justify the existence of restaurant critics.

Whole business models need a rethink in the age of Uber Eats and Deliveroo. But so too does what makes a restaurant precious: the idea that to be cooked for, to socialise and converse in a hospitable place, is something we should justify not in terms of economics or even taste, but in terms of culture and community.

The Covid-19 lockdown created a very unique experiment. For the first time in history, the majority of the people were left with the majority of their income but the lights of the high street, its restaurants and its shops, were turned off. And this posed a very profound question – what would we miss most? For business owners like me, the question is central to our very existence. Before lockdown, you see, the warning to restaurateurs and shop owners was that the world was moving online. Strategists and seminars up and down the country spoke one dark word: innovation. And innovation was essentially moving the heart of the high street to a life online, doing away with the need for face-to-face, humble human exchange. Click and collect, delivery, online films, online shopping, Zoom meetings. People, we were told, would no longer use the high street, its cinemas, its coffee shops, its clothes shops.

In every sense, a new and contactless world was what we must look forward to. There was enormous pressure on me to start a pact with a delivery company to send out what was fresh and fragrant in cardboard cartons, to be eaten on a lap, on a dark corduroy sofa somewhere. The lockdown looked as though it could be the nail in the coffin for high streets. Interestingly, as our high streets closed, there was really only one place we could spend our money and that was online. People gorged on myriad brown boxes of bits and bobs that, in terms of satisfaction, were as slaking as the cardboard in which they were wrapped. All the while, restaurateurs and shop owners like me, we waited with bated breath. How would people really want the world to change? Would human connection be traded for a contactless existence? Would our neighbourhoods continue to calcify into pleading, toothless grins as shutters replaced cafés and colour?

But what is actually happening is truly interesting. Many restaurants that chose to move to takeaway and delivery did not find a market eager to become couch consumers. Without knowing it or expecting it, it was the physical reality of hospitality that we were mourning above all. Memories, we realised, are not made on those couches with cardboard takeaways. Against a contactless life online, we rebelled. As shops reopened, there was almost vengeance queueing on the high street. Within hours of reopening, booking lines at restaurants crashed with the stampedes for tables. How wonderful and how encouraging the resurrection of neighbourhoods.

But to be worthy of the new world, we, as restaurateurs, must change. To weave ourselves into the routine of family life, we must rethink the way in which we operate and we must understand that our food, our greeting, our affordability must beckon our community to share tables heaving with good food, conversation, laughter. In short, heaving with all the things that are at the heart of being human.

And we must do that fairly and conscientiously. Like the trattoria model, simple menus serving beautifully executed food with affection and grace. That's the way our guests will learn to need their regular date with hospitality. Society has stopped the machine and it considers a contactless world arid and loveless. We, as humans, have ever needed to gather over food, to feel real contact with friends and strangers alike, share stories, halve burdens, all nestled in the warm, twinkling lights of our local eateries. To do so is to feel the very arm of your neighbourhood around your shoulders. This tells us, more than anything, that all's right with the world. It is this that we have missed most, and as the new dawn rises, we must rethink how it is this that we must protect the best.

KATHERINE GRAINGER

RETHINKING THE OLYMPICS

The ultimate glory of sport arises not from the athleticism or skill it displays, but from the morality it encourages. Sport derives its meaning from its revelation of character. And no character is an island, entire of itself; we reveal our characters alongside, and against, others.

The 2020 Games in Tokyo were postponed, of course; but the flame will light again. The Olympics were founded in a time of upheaval. A truce was called between warring factions. This in turn inspired George Orwell to write: 'Serious sport has nothing to do with fair play. It is bound up with hatred, jealousy, boastfulness, disregard of all rules and sadistic pleasure in witnessing violence. In other words, it is war minus the shooting.'

Sport is a kind of school: it teaches us about ourselves, and others. Just as in life generally, it makes competing demands on us that cannot always be reconciled. One is to play fair, observe rules, and be generous to opponents. Another is to strain every sinew to destroy said opponent; first, psychologically, and then, athletically. There is a glorious tension between fair play and pursuing victory. Which reminds me of something my best coaches told me as a kid: 'Only losers say it's the taking part that counts.'

If this pandemic gives us a chance to rethink how we approach things, how we can make changes for the better in our society, then I think when we see the return of the Olympics and the Paralympics, we should see it as a triumph of the human spirit.

We should remember the meaning behind the Games. The ancient Olympics started in a time of political upheaval, when a temporary truce was introduced to allow safe travel and participation. The modern Olympics designed a symbol of five interlocking rings to show the connection of our five continents. The Paralympics were born because sport and exercise were considered vital in the recovery of veterans of the Second World War with spinal injuries. The publicly stated values of both Games are deep-seated, human values. They are more than sport: they reflect humanity and society; they are a celebration of progression and passion; and, essentially, they demonstrate the importance of inclusion and bonding.

Tokyo 2020 had to be postponed because of Covid-19. The flame went out, but temporarily. The spirit of the Games is not broken; it remains strong. Crucially, the postponement has given us time to remember what it is we value and celebrate in this four-yearly event. The scale may have to be reduced when the Games return, but that could make it even more about the heart and spirit of competition, even more about global friendships. Athletes from all over the world connecting, countries reuniting. We will remember the simplicity of inspiration and impact, not counted in the number of fireworks lit, but in the number of hearts touched.

In a world rocked by conflicts and challenges, sport remains a place of hope that schools us in human values. It shows the importance of the pursuit of excellence and the power of the volunteer. It teaches how to face defeat and victory and learn from both. It binds competition with friendship, ambition with enjoyment and individual achievement with team unity. Over the past year, athletes around the world have laid down their training equipment, picked up new roles and embraced different perspectives. They have seized the opportunity to support others, many acknowledging inequality and seeking to address it. They will soon return to their training and will, again, have their unique power to capture the imagination of us all.

I hope soon to hear again the spine-tingling roar of the crowd and feel the visceral passion of the public at sporting events. Perhaps for a while yet more of the crowds must remain at home but I hope the Games could nevertheless connect even more deeply with the public. These events are, ultimately, a reminder of how we – united – can overcome and triumph together. How we can rebuild and refocus. We can move from separation and isolation, back to connection and inclusion. The Olympic and Paralympic Games are a moment in time. From the challenging time we are currently in, what a moment it could be. The Greatest Show on Earth will be back and the flame will burn brightly once more.

David Graeber

RETHINKING
JOBS

'The more obviously your work benefits other people, the less they pay you.' This line, my favourite from Rethink, confronts the irony of the phrase 'key workers.' Bullshit Jobs author David Graeber then shows that many people believe that if they stopped working, it would make no difference. It reminds me of a scene from the Ricky Gervais comedy The Office, when Martin Freeman's character – a sales rep at a regional branch of Wernham Hogg Paper Merchants – is asked what he does for a living. He knows his title – but can't say what the actual purpose of his job is. Can you?

It's always struck me that in the evolution of our economies from agrarian to industrial to knowledge-based to, now, a data economy, we were running out of things to manufacture. Hence a lot of people manufacturing, and selling, usually in a nice suit and with rounded vowels. This is widely known as 'management consultancy'.

Graeber died shortly after filing this essay. You can argue against him that it is vital to have people occupied for several *hours of the day instead of lying idle; and that, if people are being paid for something, there may be demand for it. Satisfying demand is generally useful.*

Our society is addicted to work. If there's anything that left and right both seem to agree on it's that jobs are always good. Everyone should have a job. Work has become our badge of moral citizenship. We seem to have convinced ourselves as a society that anyone who isn't working harder than they would like to be working at something they don't enjoy is a bad, unworthy person. As a result, work comes to absorb ever greater proportions of our energy and time. Much of this work is entirely pointless.

Whole industries; think telemarketers, corporate law, private equity. Whole lines of work: middle management, brand strategists, high-level hospital or school administrators, editors of inhouse corporate magazines. All exist primarily to convince us that there is some reason for their existence. Useless work crowds out useful; think your teachers and nurses overwhelmed with paperwork. It's also almost invariably better compensated. As we've seen in lockdown, the more obviously your work benefits other people, the less they pay you. The system makes no sense. It's also destroying the planet.

If we don't break ourselves of this addiction quickly, we will leave our children and grandchildren to face catastrophes on a scale that will make the current pandemic seem trivial. If what I'm saying isn't obvious, the main reason is that we're constantly encouraged to look at social problems as if they were questions of personal morality. All this work, all the carbon we're pouring into the atmosphere must somehow be the result of our consumerism. Therefore, we need to stop eating meat or stop dreaming of flying off to beach vacations, but this is just wrong. It's not our pleasures that are destroying the world, it's our puritanism, our feeling that we have to suffer in order to deserve those pleasures.

If we really want to save the world we're going to have to stop working so much. Seventy per cent of greenhouse gas emissions worldwide come from infrastructure, energy, transport, construction. Most of the rest is produced by industry. Meanwhile, 37 per cent of British workers feel if their jobs were to disappear it would make no difference whatsoever. Simply do the math. These workers are right. We could massively reduce climate change just by eliminating bullshit jobs. So, that's my proposal number one. Eliminate bullshit jobs.

Proposal number two. Batshit construction. An enormous amount of building today is purely speculative. All over the world governments collude with the financial sector to create glittering towers that are never occupied; empty office buildings, airports that are never used. Stop doing this. No one will miss them.

Proposal three. Planned obsolescence. One of the main reasons we have such high levels of industrial production is that we design everything to break or at the very least to become outmoded and useless in a few years' time. If you build an iPhone to break in three years, you can sell five times as many than if you made it to last 15, but you're also using five times the resources and creating five times the pollution and waste. Manufacturers are perfectly capable of making iPhones or stockings or lightbulbs that wouldn't break. In fact, they actually do make them, they're called military grade. Force manufacturers to make military grade products for everyone. We could cut down greenhouse gas production massively and improve our quality of life.

These three suggestions are just for starters. If you think about it, they're really just common sense. Why destroy the world if you don't have to? If addressing them seems unrealistic, you might do well to think hard about what those realities are that seem to be forcing us as a society to behave in ways that are literally mad.

JAMES HARDING

RETHINKING
NEWS

*Aside from the eloquence of the prose, and the authority of the
writer, what makes James Harding's essay on rethinking news
so powerful is its application of a recent lesson from the world
of politics to journalism.*

Harding was the youngest ever editor of The Times, *at
38. He went on to be director of BBC News, before founding
Tortoise Media, which is dedicated to slow journalism – that
is, news when it's ready.*

*I said in the introduction that of all the paradigms for
politics that explain our present predicament, fast vs slow
was perhaps the most apposite. With Tortoise Media, Harding applied that dichotomy to journalism, trying to get away
from the frenetic noise of social media, to the actual news that
matters. In this essay, he in effect applies another paradigm
that has become popular of late: Anywhere vs Somewhere.*

*Popularised by the writer David Goodhart, this asserts that
belonging, and attachment to place, is the enduring human
need to which recent politics has failed to give sufficient weight.*

A majority of people aren't hyper-mobile jet setters, but rather members of a stable community who live relatively close to where they grew up. Rootedness is sacred.

Yet the journalistic expression of this – local newspapers – has taken a battering the whole world over, as the classified adverts that once funded it have shifted online, along with their readership. Harding reports that the pandemic has prompted hope for revival in this area of decline, as a variety of business models emerge, each accepting the premise that quality costs.

The idea that we should think of journalism as a branch of geography is profound. As he says in his wider analysis, the 'pandemic has revealed more than it has changed'; but where it has changed things, it may have given us hope. Journalism matters more than ever. And if 'life is local', as many a local paper once boasted, then this essay is as perspicacious as it is optimistic.

The pandemic has given us plenty of reasons to change our minds – whether it's about Piers Morgan, press conferences or the *Daily Star*'s front page. And, when it comes to journalism, the coronavirus has forced me to rethink regional news.

Covid-19 has been a story often best covered by maps and stats: we have plugged in our postcode on the ONS's interactive map and tracked infection and hospitalisation rates in our region because it's relevant. More and more, we turn to the Nextdoor app for the hyperlocal news or the neighbourhood WhatsApp group for the community information that really matters to us.

Whereas journalists tend to turn to historical precedent to explain a story, this time we have reached for the heatmaps that show the inequality of illness, death and treatment between countries, within countries and across cities and counties. The topography of the pandemic has forced us to see our country more honestly.

We have, of course, been mourning the death of local newspapers for 30 years. More local reporting jobs have gone in the pandemic; in the last few months, local newspaper groups have been sold off like broken toys at charity-shop prices. And regional TV news, the one place where regional reporting has commanded a mass audience, now has it coming: its numbers are going to be eroded by the exodus of viewers from broadcasters like the BBC and ITV to streamers like Netflix, Amazon and Disney+.

Let's not be naïve. News deserts are a reality in the UK as well as the US. Stamping our feet about the importance of local news to the health of our democracy has proved as useful as a rain dance. And recent history gives no grounds for optimism. Devolution to Scotland and Wales was supposed to reinvigorate journalism there. But Wales is one of our driest news deserts; Scotland's hardly lush. Just because there's a greater need to provide information or hold power to account doesn't mean that it happens. Timothy Snyder, the Yale historian, points to the decline in local news as one of the preconditions of post-truth the world over. For a long while now, local news has been journalism's favourite lost cause.

But, this year, there have been concrete, commercial reasons to believe things will change. The pandemic has demonstrated consumer demand for news and information based on where you are, whether you're turning to the evening bulletin, a website, newsletter or local app. And businesses have shown a renewed financial interest in regional news services, both as a platform to advertise their commitment to the area and a marketplace for reaching the customers who live there.

The news industry is simultaneously re-engineering the business model, whether it's newsletters operating on low costbases like *The Charlotte Agenda* in North Carolina or *The Mill* in Manchester; or subscription news businesses like *The Athletic* or local bloggers on Substack signing up paying customers locally.

We're a long way from singing hallelujah. These innovations will not be the saving of the local newspaper business. The market town may be too small a market to sustain a digital news business. But this long year has made it plausible to think that the metro area – a city and its surroundings – can once again be a marketplace for the new news media as much as it is a power base in politics.

Devolution used to be the obsession of only a rarefied species of wonk. It's a mainstream sport now. The battles over test and trace, Covid compensation and the vaccination rollout between Downing Street, on the one hand, and Manchester, Birmingham, Liverpool, London, the North East and the South West have stoked a different kind of campaign for taking back control. The metro mayors are emboldened. We've seen the need for checks and balances on the centre. Regional competitiveness is on the agenda. Power and resources in the post-pandemic decade will, in one form or another, flow to the regions – and, with it, stories, resources and the requirement for regional journalism that holds those in power to account and gives people what they want to know.

The pandemic year has tended to reinforce our convictions in the things we already thought in the first place: in my case, the UK constitution is rickety and muddled, the internet is dangerously lawless and exams seem increasingly divorced from education. That's because the pandemic has revealed more than it has changed. The generation gap. The global gap between East and West. The income and education gap. The power gap between the centre and the regions.

It's shown that the map of journalism itself is unhealthy. There's inequality of information, as well as incomes and opportunity. The arguments against excessive centralism in our government have rung true in the news media too.

Journalism, as the *Washington Post* publisher Phil Graham famously said, is 'the first rough draft of history'. In the past year, I've come to think it might be better as a branch of geography. For the first time in a long time, there's reason to believe that regional news can come out of this fitter and stronger. More and more people want information that's closer to home – the news not defined by politics and party stripe, but by place.

Carolyn McCall

RETHINKING
TELEVISION

What, after all, is the role of the media in a society? Three things, I'd say: to inform the citizenry, apply scrutiny to power and enlighten our culture. The last of these is broad, of course, and in my definition it includes entertaining people and providing a common well of emotional resources from which all can draw.

Among the great institutions of our media, few do these better, or in a bigger way, than ITV. And yet as its chief executive Carolyn McCall argues in this essay, its ability to do this has in some ways been compromised by the astonishing growth of the data kings of California. At the highest level, the richest companies in human history are now competing for our ears and eyeballs in the attention economy. Even just two decades ago, ITV didn't have to think about that.

And there is a smaller, more specific way in which the data kings are diminishing what are known as Britain's public service broadcasters (PSBs). Since the likes of Apple or Amazon now control the interfaces through which we watch television, *they are able to favour their own shows in the digital shop windows they own. Nearly 20 years ago, Britain passed legislation to guarantee prominence to PSBs, because they provide benefits to society. That legislation, McCall argues, is hopelessly out of date.*

There is a profound danger that our culture becomes homogenised, or Americanised: that the vast bulk of the shows we watch are ultimately controlled from California. This is not a sensible place for any nation to be. Covid-19 showed that the precious ecology of British broadcast and digital media – what Tim Davie, the director-general of the BBC, called an 'enlightened blend' – is cherished by people across the country. They want news they can trust and shows that reflect life in Britain in all its glory, as part of the infinite menu of content we all have before us today. McCall makes the case well.

The Covid-19 pandemic has accelerated the fundamental structural changes already transforming the broadcast industry in the UK. People's viewing habits are changing as they move to digital platforms and internet-connected TVs. Much of the focus of viewers and commentators has been on the output of the US online streaming players and their vast financial resources.

That's understandable: it's what we view. However, it's the global online platforms – Google, Amazon and others – that we increasingly view our favoured content through that will have the greater impact longer term.

Their ambition is to 'own the home' and with it as much household expenditure and advertising revenue as they can secure.

Their operating systems and services support multiple devices and are easy for consumers to use, with features such as voice control, personalisation and single billing. As well as capturing consumer data these systems provide income from their owned services but also demand a share of third-party revenues as well – such as subscription to other providers, shared advertising income, payments for access and prominence.

Typically, they start negotiations for access to their platforms by demanding a share of any subscription revenue and one third of advertising revenue or an equivalent amount of inventory. By that I mean the right to sell the advertising space direct to brands and agencies, thus not only reducing your ad revenue but building their own ad sales business.

Amazon's most recent trading figures reveal their increasing domination. The year 2020 saw Amazon achieving earning net sales of $386 billion. That's up 38 per cent on 2019 and Amazon now accounts for an estimated £1 of every £20 spent in the UK's retail sector.

Although these online platforms are increasingly offering content like sport and drama, that's less about diversifying into television on demand and much more about growing sales of their other products to customers.

What does this mean for the UK's public service broadcasters – known as PSBs – the BBC, ITV and Channels 4 and 5? In the not-too-distant future they will increasingly find that they will only be able to get their programmes to households in the UK via those platforms. Left unchecked, the powerful owners of those platforms will be able to dictate terms that could kill off PSBs in their current guise in favour of their own services and other global streamers with whom they have done worldwide deals.

This is not about a fear of competition. Far from it: our industry is built on intense competition. But it's about competing on a level playing field. At the moment we are playing the game with a rule book (devised in 2003) enforced by a strict referee against an opposition that chooses which rules to follow.

This is the backdrop for a fundamental rethink of the TV landscape that has been going on at Ofcom, the media industry regulator. The result of its deliberations – and the government's response – will have an impact not just on the future of the public service media and the broader creative economy but on our society at large.

One thing that the Covid pandemic has illustrated very clearly is the vital importance of a national system of broadcasting and media, with live news, local information and entertainment reflecting our cultures, our experience, our politics and our society. It has been the PSBs that have risen to the challenge of delivering this. Despite the most formidable obstacles, they have informed the public about the pandemic fairly and impartially while also offering them an escape from it through their dramas and entertainment shows.

Just before Christmas 2020, Ofcom set out its thoughts on the future of the PSBs. The headline was that the UK media sector is a success story, with public service broadcasting at its core. It is a vibrant, thriving part of the economy and the PSBs are the heart of the system. No other country has this blend or breadth of public and commercial companies. Public service broadcasting brings people together by creating shared national experiences as well as reflecting the UK's diversity across its nations and regions.

What I found so encouraging from the Ofcom report were the voices of ordinary people talking about what the channels mean to them. They really are a vital part of our national life and Ofcom's research showed that audiences of all ages and demographics value what PSBs bring, not only to them as individuals, but more broadly in connecting generations and society as a whole through coverage of events and programmes watched by many millions.

Let me be clear that we're not afraid of competition or of change. We're embracing both. At ITV we know that we've got to respond and we're doing so. We're investing at scale in ITV Hub, we're partnering with the BBC on

BritBox, and our Studios business is creating and selling shows to both broadcasters and streaming platforms around the world. But what Ofcom now calls Public Service Media needs a fair and level playing field on which to compete.

At its heart, this is about ensuring that people can continue to easily find and access the highest quality national and global TV services. It shouldn't be one or the other – people want both. But the system we operate is a creation of legislation which is almost 20 years old and urgently needs a radical update. There has been a digital revolution but we still have an analogue regulatory framework for media.

If we have learned anything from the pandemic it is that people prize the programmes the PSBs offer and a key part of the government's Build Back Better agenda must be to create a viable framework for a new PSB system.

After the year we've had, the people of this country deserve it.

HOW
WE
FEEL

MOHAMMED HANIF

RETHINKING INTIMACY

*What, when you think about it, have you most missed during
lockdown? For most people, even if they don't realise it, the
answer is probably physical contact with other human beings.
In the British-Pakistani writer Mohammed Hanif's home city
of Karachi and many other places, intimacy can have a trans-
gressive quality. And yet in other parts of the world, perhaps
the bigger issue was the lack of physical touch altogether.*

*As I wrote in the introduction, many societies, and
perhaps especially those in what we loosely term the West,
are experiencing a crisis of connection. By this, I don't mean
the wifi is dodgy. Rather, atomised souls deprived of love are
– literally – dying from want of it. In the US and Britain,
the decades-long rise in life expectancy had reversed even
before Covid-19. Deaths of despair were rising. It is trite to
say, in response to this, that what those who suffer from, say,
alcoholism most need is a hug. It is not trite, however, to say
that what they need is love. And intimacy is the physical
expression of love.*

I suspect that parents around the world will relate, with a wry smile or roll of the eyes, to Hanif's image of a young boy hunting dinosaur bones on a beach. I for one am grateful for one thing above all in this pandemic: the liberty to hug – that is, be intimate – with my own dinosaur-obsessed son.

We built humanity by touching each other, with hugs and air kisses and handshakes. And not just with people we like and love and care about. Civilisation was forged through double handshakes with our enemies and embraces with our potential killers. Love has always been a kiss under the barrel of a gun and fingers touching through iron bars. Will we ever learn to be intimate the way we used to be? Will we ever sneak up behind a long-lost friend and cover their eyes with our hands and whisper, 'Guess who?' Will they turn around and slap us or just say, 'Oh, you again.' Will we ever nod off onto the fellow passenger's shoulder? Will we ever be able to do running reviews into a friend's ear while watching a play? Actually, will there ever be theatre and rehearsals and those confidence-building exercises where you shut your eyes and fall, expecting your fellow actors to catch you? Maybe we all wore masks before and now we are wearing masks over our masks.

We were worried about our children, them being knifed at school or abused. But now I worry that should I stand guard with a sanitiser over my child's head, so that no stranger dare tousle his beautiful hair? Even before Covid, I spent a lot of time spurning the world. Some days, I felt that the world is exactly where I wanted it to be, at a safe distance away.

Maybe we had too much intimacy. Universities were installing cameras on campuses to catch students making out. Maybe there was too much public display of affection. Why were we hugging strangers at funerals of people we found irritating when they were alive? Why were we patting cheeks of cute children in parks? Now that parks are shut, every afternoon, we go and visit a kitten who lives inside a beauty salon. We read somewhere that kittens don't do Corona. Kittens make us feel safe but we still carry our sanitisers in our pockets.

Are we too scared? Because there are others who are fearless. The beauty salon is under lockdown but people still sneak in and get beauty things done. Monday, I saw a fully made-up bride emerge from the salon. She wore red silk and lots of jewellery, her companion wore a mask and gloves. The bride seemed eager to get into the car and start her new intimate life.

In Karachi, we live near a polluted beach. This is where my wife and I had first kissed, many years ago. It was unexpected; we weren't planning to. That random kiss led to a life together. Last week, we dared to venture out to the same beach with our six-year-old son. Bored of his online classes and YouTube binges, he wanted to go digging for dinosaur bones. We all wore masks and carried our sanitisers. As we saw our son totally absorbed in his digging, we kissed with our masks on, maybe trying to re-enact our first kiss. It was funny and strangely comforting. Maybe one day, we won't be as scared as we are now.

H.R. McMaster

RETHINKING EMPATHY

Before he was briefly America's 26th National Security Advisor, under Donald Trump, Herbert Raymond McMaster was one of the outstanding soldiers of his generation. He served leading roles in the first Gulf War, and then in what was named Operation Iraqi Freedom. As a veteran of, and expert in, war – that is, methodical killing or conflict, usually in the service of a country or tribe – he has spent decades patrolling moral as well as national boundaries.

In McMaster's telling, empathy is the foundation of morality. Moral analysis and consideration can only begin when I recognise that you matter. Not merely that you exist, but that your preferences and feelings deserve respect. In this way, empathy, that ability to feel or understand someone else, is the instinctive prelude to sympathy, the ability to feel pity, sorrow or compassion for someone else. Sympathy spreads in dwindling waves from the self to the outside world.

One function of journalism is to bring the far-away near, so that the moral needs of those we don't know personally

are impressed upon our senses. In McMaster's telling of it,
much of public life today militates against our nurturing of
the empathy that is the foundation of a better world.

Anger over a policeman's atrocious murder of Mr George Floyd and the protests and violence that erupted in the midst of a pandemic, laid bare deep divisions in America and democracies around the world. Those divisions are widening. A lack of empathy for one another is catalysing a destructive interaction between identity politics, vitriolic partisan rhetoric, bigotry and racism. Lack of empathy is rooted in ignorance and unwillingness to listen. Those who are strangers to their fellow citizens seek affirmation of their biases rather than mutual understanding. I propose that we cultivate empathy for each other to change the world and strengthen democracy. We can empathise with one another by considering how our past produced frustrations of the present. A historical perspective on current divisions can help us generate empathy based not on a contrived, happy view of history but on the recognition that experiments in freedom and democracy are works in progress.

Indeed, the emancipation of 4 million people after the most destructive war in American history was only the beginning of a long journey for equal rights. A journey that is not over. In America, citizens can demand change because our republic was founded on the idea that sovereignty lies with the people. Our government derives just powers from the consent of the governed. Citizens of free and open societies can drive change through the pursuit of true equality of opportunity as we rebuild trust in institutions, improve education, strengthen families and close the widening gap between the haves and the have-nots.

Empathy for one another can help us recognise, as America's founders did, that our democracies require constant nurturing and improvement. As we confront a pandemic, global recession and civil unrest, a narrative has emerged that authoritarian systems are superior to democracies. We should remember the concentration camps in China and bear witness to the Communist Party's extension of its cyber-enabled police state to stifle freedom across the country and now in Hong Kong. We should be confident the citizens of democracies have a voice. If we truly listen, and cultivate empathy, we can work together to strengthen and improve our democracies. We can build a better world. As the American civil rights activist and patriot, Rosa Parks, observed, to bring about change, you must not be afraid to take the first step. We will fail when we fail to try.

CAROL COOPER

RETHINKING RACIAL EQUALITY

Carol Cooper spent years championing the complex and often misunderstood ideas of diversity and inclusion long before they were fashionable. She asks us to rethink racial equality – not racism.

Most people know what racism is – discrimination on the basis of race – and would instinctively consider it wrong. Racial equality is a much harder idea, because it packages together two of the most loaded and philosophically swollen words in the English language. Race is more of a socially deployed than scientifically coherent concept. Equality is similarly extremely difficult to define; and, because people are so unequal, achieving more equal outcomes often requires treating people unequally.

The extent to which Cooper has been affected by George Floyd's death, and shaped by her father's experience as part of the Windrush generation, is clear. And I do wonder if one consequence of recent events is that, in pursuit of greater equality and justice, we rethink the phrase BAME. It seems so absurd to lump together so many different ethnic communities, given their wildly different situations, just because it forms an acronym with vowels in convenient locations. Much better, when talking about different ethnicities, to be as specific as possible.

The history of 400 years played out for the world to see in 8 minutes and 46 seconds, when Mr George Floyd pleaded, 'I can't breathe.'

The US carried out its subjugation largely on its own shores and have had to live in the shadows of its sins, while perpetuating the reality that the lines of the poem written by Emma Lazarus – which cries with silent lips, 'Give me your tired, your poor, / Your huddled masses yearning to breathe free' – were not meant for the descendants of slaves, because 'we can't breathe.'

The UK has the luxury of distance from the plantations that funded their largesse, but the data and lived experiences of thousands bear witness that racism is quite literally killing us. We also cry, 'We can't breathe.'

But, like Claude McKay:

If we must die, let it not be like hogs,
Hunted and penned in an inglorious spot.
While round us bark the mad and hungry dogs
Making their mock at our accursèd lot.
If we must die, O let us nobly die,
So that our precious blood may not be shed

In vain; then even the monsters we defy,
Shall be constrained to honour us though dead!

My father, a Windrush pioneer, arrived in the UK in 1948 to a motherland who we now know had not intended the 'coloureds' to help it rebuild after the war. In 2020, the word 'Windrush' is a reminder of the many who are still waiting for compensation for the injustices to which the faceless, unaccountable system subjected them.

Mr George Floyd's dying words are most certainly the epitome of 'the worst of times', but thousands of people risking their safety in the middle of a pandemic to shout in the streets, 'No justice, no peace!' awakens the cry of the slave, the colonised, the victims of racism, who are still saying, 'We can't breathe.' The coming together of peoples of all races signalled hope that we may be on the eve of 'the best of times'.

We have a moment, a whisper of time to consider whether we plaster over these open wounds of our history and our present or whether we, the sons and daughters of the slaves and the slave masters, take down the societal and structural racism along with the statues that glorify their reign of terror or whether we continue to give life to the spirit of the slave catcher in our midst who holds us in abeyance under the knee.

In 2020, black people are over four times more likely to die from coronavirus but we are also fighting with the more invasive and resistant virus of racism. We can decide whether justice delayed means justice denied and we can decide whether the 'colour of a man's skin is of no more significance than the colour of his eyes'.

I have a dream that the post-Covid, new-normal world is one in which institutional racism is rendered to history. Healing from racial injustice needs truth and reconciliation at a societal, institutional and personal level.

On 1 August 1834, as the sun dawned in Jamaica, the praying slaves ran to the top of the hills to meet the rising sun that signalled their freedom.

In 2020, we are, black and white, standing at the base of those hills and saying to Mr Boris Johnson and his government: you now have a moment in time to start the healing from the trauma of slavery, colonialism and racism. A spiritual renewing that will enable us all to breathe. Justice points the way to a new normal, a life without institutional racism. So, please, 'sir', let the healing begin, just let us breathe ...

Paul Krugman

RETHINKING
SOLIDARITY

Paul Krugman made his name with exceptionally wonkish and innovative economic thinking. For this he won the Nobel Prize. In the past two decades, he has reinvented himself. Still a wonk, but also the self-avowed conscience of a liberal, in the American sense. He wants America to have a new, better social contract, underpinned by a smart, effective state. Moreover, one that imposes more duties than it does rights on the American people.

Krugman points out something peculiar, even salutary, about Covid-19. Unlike other crises, this one isn't anyone's fault. Sure, it originated in China. But, contrary to the conspiracies that abound in corners of the internet, there were no dark forces that spread the virus. It was a very unhappy accident. This should force us to recognise our inescapable interdependence. That in turn should help us understand that, just as no individual started this crisis, no individual can end it, or rebuild our world after it. Only societies can, with the help of effective government.

Will there be any silver lining to Covid-19? Will it change the world for the better? The answer, of course, is that we don't know. But if we learn the right lessons from this global trauma, the world could emerge as a better place for there is something to learn from this pandemic: namely that we are, whether we like it or not, our brother's keepers. The coronavirus has made an overwhelming case for more social solidarity in several different ways.

First, Covid-19 has created a crisis that is nobody's fault. That's a bigger deal than you might imagine. Whenever things go wrong, many of us, me too, tend to look for someone to blame and perhaps punish. All our problems, many are tempted to argue, are caused by ... take your pick. Evil foreigners, people whose skin colour is different, greedy capitalists or vast conspiracies of ruthless cosmopolitans. And of course, some people, including people with real power, insist on trying to squeeze the pandemic into that frame. My own government has been trying desperately to rename it the Chinese Virus. But zero-sum thinking, the attempt to blame villains you can punish, just doesn't work for this problem. This is a threat we all face and it requires a cooperative solution.

Second, it turns out that responding well to the coronavirus requires not just that governments act, but that individuals do their part. Simple acts of responsibility, like wearing a mask in public, turn out to make a huge difference in a way that, say, individual attempts to reduce your carbon footprint probably don't. In this crisis, in other words, achieving a decent social outcome requires that we act decently and thoughtfully as individuals, which seems to me to be a good lesson for everyone to learn. And while there are people and political factions who angrily reject calls to behave decently, that's a useful lesson too. We have a chance to see these people and factions for who they truly are.

Finally, when it comes to government policy, this pandemic is a kind of object lesson in the reality of the social compact. On one side, it's helpful, I believe, to see the importance of hanging together in the face of a threat that isn't military, that doesn't come from a foreign power or anything like that. Pandemic control reveals that there really is such a thing as the common good, which requires that we act together in our mutual interest.

And we're also seeing that the social safety net really is protection for all of us. While the coronavirus has, on average, hurt the poor more than the rich, its impact has a huge amount of randomness and not just in terms of who gets infected. Some jobs have disappeared while others are unscathed, which I think will mean that in the future, it will be easier to make the case that a strong safety net protects everyone. So, my hope is that this episode will make us more willing to accept the notion that we're a society, not just individuals. And that we are all better off if we take seriously our obligations to each other.

AMONGE SINXOTO

RETHINKING SAFETY

Those of us who live in relative comfort and security in the West need regular reminding that for hundreds of millions of people around the world, the experience of life is the experience of constant danger.

South African youth activist Amonge Sinxoto marshals shocking statistics that make clear just how threatening daily life in many parts of the world are. Not least her native country, of course. Parts of South Africa have a justified reputation as being amongst the most dangerous places to live in the world. But the issue of physical safety, and the lack thereof, is particularly acute for women. In the West, the feminist struggle has won important victories in terms of rights, representation and equality – though there is still a huge amount to do. In many parts of the world, the struggle has begun, but the most basic victories are a very long way from sight.

It was back in 1995 that Hillary Clinton, then First Lady of the United States, and one of the most important feminist icons of the past century, gave a speech in Beijing at which she argued that women's rights are human rights. That speech won huge plaudits for its courage and clarity. A quarter of a century on, listening to Sinxoto, you'd be forgiven for thinking not nearly enough has changed.

I am Amonge Elethu Sinxoto, a teenager, social entrepreneur and activist from Johannesburg, South Africa. I have been thinking about what progress might look like post-Covid-19. How would the world have changed for the better, if at all? The buzz phrase that has been making the rounds is 'new normal'. Everyone is talking about the changes that the Covid-19 pandemic is going to introduce to our society. I think the pandemic has forced all of us to stop in our tracks, and it has emphasised the urgent need to address some of the most pressing social issues.

I thought about my own experience as a woman living in a country with one of the world's highest rape statistics, coupled with abysmal conviction rates. This reality has characterised my existence for many years, living in a world where I am not safe as a woman in my social context. Every day there is a new story about a woman being abused, raped or killed, and I am constantly confronted by the fear that I might be next. As a society, living in this endless loop of violence has forced us to be complacent and desensitised to women's reality across South Africa.

It has been interesting to see the urgency with which the world closed up shop to prioritise the preservation of life. However, it makes me sad to know that the pandemic of systemic racism has plagued black people in the United States for hundreds of years, with nothing as swift and decisive being done to mitigate the problem. The pattern of police brutality and excessive use of force, particularly towards black and brown individuals resulting in severe injury and very often death, has been their 'normal'. Their lives can be taken at a moment's notice by the very people who are authorised to serve and protect them. In what is supposed to be the greatest nation on earth, a child playing with a toy gun is not safe; going for a run in your neighbourhood is not safe. Even while sleeping in your own house, you're not safe simply because of your skin colour; this is a pandemic that the world has ignored for far too long.

Women in South Africa have also been living in a pandemic for years. Forty per cent of women in South Africa are predicted to experience some form of sexual assault in their lifetime. There were 42,289 reported rapes in 2019/2020, which means an average of 116 rapes each day. They are left at the mercy of a police system riddled with corruption and bribery that enables the problem to continue with zero or little repercussions for the perpetrators. It is estimated that just 14 per cent of perpetrators of rape are convicted in South Africa. That is a pandemic! Where is the same urgency for the preservation of life? Where are the stringent measures in place? Where are the voices that should say 'everything will stop so that we can eradicate this problem'?

As we talk about progress and what the future looks like, we should bear in mind two things. The first is that we must listen and understand the injustices in our world, have a moment of reflection, and educate ourselves about these issues. The second thing we must consider is what happens after Covid-19 when our lives return to 'normal'. When we go back to hanging out with friends, public events and life without face masks. The conversation around these issues and the pursuit of solutions has to remain a priority. The real test of progress is the action and initiatives that come after awareness is created.

Progress is policy reform.

Progress is education.

Progress is change.

Progress is when the 'new normal' entails preservation of all life for ALL.

REED HASTINGS
RETHINKING TOGETHERNESS

No company in the history of entertainment or media has changed so much so fast as the one Reed Hastings founded: Netflix.

Twenty-first-century media is fragmenting as never before. In the mid-twentieth century, when there were relatively few sources of news or entertainment, ratings for some shows were huge. They brought nations together. In the internet age, choice is virtually infinite, so we inevitably spend more time in our own information and entertainment universes. Until the likes of Netflix came along. So strong and convenient is its offer that Netflix and other streaming giants are reviving an older idea of media. Not just as a source of fascination and fun, but as the essence of a civilised public domain that shapes the temper of a people.

Ultimately, as Hastings suggests, the stories that have the greatest appeal – and that are most effective at bringing us together – are those whose characters, plots and moral teachings instinctively strike us as universal.

Throughout history, moments of intense crisis usually result in one of two outcomes. A cultural reawakening, a renewal of the timeless ideas of solidarity, community and togetherness. Or a retreat, an entrenchment into ourselves, shutting out the pressures and challenges we face, erecting barriers and borders in the physical world and in our minds. There is no telling where we'll land on this scale. I think we can all hope for the former, but also sympathise with the latter. Understanding that it's an incredibly natural, human instinct.

I can relate. Throughout this pandemic, I have missed being around the incredible team we've built at Netflix over the past 20-plus years. I've missed my friends, my kids and my wider family even more. At moments like this (I am writing this in June 2020), you just want to be with the people you care about, batten down the hatches and keep those closest to you safe. But as we emerge from this crisis, if we want to see real change, for the better, we must look beyond our own backyards and beyond our own immediate concerns. We need to find a way to nurture and sustain the sense of togetherness that has been such a positive by-product of this terrible time. This pandemic has impacted us all but it has impacted some communities far more profoundly than others. And in too many cases, its effects will continue to be felt for years to come.

As governments, societies and individuals, we must start to adjust for a new world order. And we must do that in the wake not just of a pandemic, but also of an important global movement targeting social inequality and injustice. Against that backdrop, it has never felt more important for humanity to find common ground, to celebrate the things that unite us, to reach for the truth about our lives that go beyond borders and connect us to a wider world. With daily life at a standstill, there has been an unusually captive audience, hungry for distraction, for entertainment, for a connection with the outside world.

In that context, entertainment providers have a vital role to play in fostering a better understanding of other people's lives by offering up films, series and documentaries that can help audiences find common ground. I've always believed that what you find on Netflix and what you see on our screens more broadly, should be a reflection of the real world, in all its astounding, complex glory. And that means sometimes uncovering the most uncomfortable and challenging parts of our society. Championing unheard causes and creating content that goes against the grain of what's typically exported by Hollywood. We know that great stories can come from anywhere and be loved everywhere. And we have made it our mission to work with the best storytellers from all around the world and give them a global platform.

Throughout the pandemic, we've seen our members watching more content from other countries or cultures. In part, that's because people have had more time to explore our service, in part it's because we're discovering that the more global we become, the more important it is that we work with local, diverse creators, to tell local, authentic stories that speak to us all. Shows like La Casa de Papel from our team in Spain, Unorthodox from Germany and Summertime in Italy. These stories translate across borders because they reflect universal truths. At their best, stories have the power to make a real impact in people's lives. Thirteen, Orange Is the New Black, When They See Us, Roma – that is how we change the world.

For all the trauma and pain Covid-19 has caused and will continue to cause, this collective experience has also the potential to help us re-evaluate how much we have in common. Sharing in each other's cultures and stories means we can better relate to each other and feel closer together.

My hope for the post-Covid world is that we will hold on to that sense of togetherness. That more people will engage with stories that challenge our world view. That we will redouble our commitment to telling stories that build empathy, inspire action and ultimately unite us.

RETHINKING ACCOUNTABILITY

It's a big call, but perhaps no country in the world has dealt with Covid-19 as well as South Korea. Historians will have to be the judge of that. Nobody today could seriously doubt, however, that the country's effective leadership and competent government have lessons for the rest of us.

Which is why it is so striking that Kang Kyung-wha, the first woman to be foreign minister of South Korea – a democracy historically and geographically attached to a nuclear dictatorship – should choose accountability as her subject.

She argues that accountability can only be secured through the two 'T's: trust and transparency. Trust, like all social benefits, is easily destroyed but not easily created. For a variety of reasons, many cultural, some demographic, South Korean society has a very high degree of trust.

Mix this with a culture of transparency, in which the workings of government are open, and politicians are willing to admit when they screw things up, and you might get a healthy democracy. That is, a system of representation in which the people know what is being done on their behalf. For all the (justified) talk of a democratic recession, or correction, in recent years – and the tendency to append such chatter to the rise of China – it is worth noting that one of the best adverts for democracy is the nation barely a thousand kilometres east of Beijing. And there are few better adverts for South Korea than the remarkable Kang Kyung-wha.

Covid-19 has tested the ability of governments to perform our most basic duty, which is to protect the safety and dignity of our peoples. For democracies, it has also tested our ability to do so while being faithful to our values. Foremost among these is accountability to the people who give governments the responsibility and the power to govern. It is perhaps easy to brush this aside when struck by crisis, when there is little time and governments are pressed for immediate action. But in fact crisis is a time for democracies to redouble our commitment to accountability. And the best way to do so is to be transparent. Full disclosure about what the government is doing or not doing in the midst of a crisis may be difficult, but it is all the more critical for this is the only way to win the public's trust, which is the most important ingredient in effective crisis management.

The public needs to be informed and assured that the government is doing its very best to serve them. In Korea we have tenaciously stuck to this commitment from the very beginning of Covid-19. Every day we have shared with the public what we know and don't know, what we are doing or not doing about the fast-spreading disease. And we did so based on science and evidence, continuously adapting our measures in line with the growing body of knowledge about this tricky virus, and we did so even at times when government action was falling short and we were faced with severe criticism. In turn, public trust in government generated civic participation and social distancing and civic activism in solutions that complemented government measures in testing, tracing and treatment.

A clear confirmation of this trust was the highest voter turnout in nearly three decades for the elections in mid-April 2020. Crises tend to turn countries insular and reveal the weakest links in our societies. Across the world, Covid-19 has prompted governments to close borders and weakened the solidarity that is needed to overcome global challenges. Inside countries, it has exposed deep-seated inequalities, lacks in state capacity, the pitfalls of technology and many more tough problems. Democracies must face up to these with honesty and humility and join forces for the dignity and safety of all of humanity. Only by doing so will we be stronger and better prepared to grapple with today's and tomorrow's challenges.

LUCY JONES

RETHINKING BIOPHILIA

One of the recurring themes of these Rethink essays is the idea that lockdown has created an opportunity for reconnecting with the natural world. Lucy Jones, the author of Losing Eden: Why Our Minds Need the Wild, wants a radical reset.

You may have already read Jarvis Cocker talk about his rediscovery of the glorious hen harrier (see page 59), or Prince Charles's manifesto for restoring harmony with nature (see page 231). Echoing and expanding on some of these themes, Jones suggests that intimately and intricately involving considerations of the natural world in all our urban and planning decisions would be better for both the natural world and for us. She lays bare the sheer state of our disconnection from natural ecosystems with some shocking statistics.

I suspect that most people would find it hard to disagree with the principle that animates her argument: a belief that our wild inheritance should be respected. Some of her suggestions are exciting: roundabouts that double up as rainforests, or industrial estates that are orchards. (Staff at the latter would *presumably be in favour.) The question is how, practically, to involve nature in our unnatural plans. That can only happen if a love of nature – biophilia – is closer to the surface of our thoughts than generally occurs today.*

While writing my book *Losing Eden: Why Our Minds Need the Wild*, I wondered whether this need for the wild might be dormant in the West. It seemed that the 'biophilia gene', the idea that we have an innate affinity to the living world, simply hadn't been triggered for many in our eco-alienated society.

The UK is one of the most nature-depleted countries in the world. Over 2.5 million people don't live within easy walking distance of a green space. Deep-rooted structures of injustice mean many feel unwelcome in natural environments. As nature declines, so too does our relationship with it.

Or so I thought.

For in lockdown, there has been a renaissance of love for nature. People found solace in the unfurling of spring. Others found companionship in nature at a time of loneliness and grief. We saw and heard things we'd never taken the time to notice before: the return of the swifts, the sound of a cuckoo.

UK visits to parks were up 67 per cent and nearly 90 per cent of people said being in nature made them happy. Retailers reported record demand for seeds. Birdsong replaced car horns. You could hear insects buzzing instead of the drone of the motorways.

Lockdown suggested to us the primal value of connecting with the wild. Now we know it feels good, but is there any evidence backing this up?

There is now a robust evidence base from scientific disciplines across the world that proves connection with nature is crucial for mental health.

From stress recovery to brain activity, the nervous system to the microbiome, the pathways are myriad. It is akin to eating vegetables or getting a good night's sleep.

So, how can we bring our lockdown-triggered biophilia into the new world?

Inequality of access to nature must be a political priority. Expecting people to live on streets without trees, or children to play in concrete squares, is a stain on our society. Nature isn't a luxury, or an add-on. Nor should it be protected simply because of what it can do for us.

We can make our neighbourhoods biophilic. We can be better co-tenants with other species. Let's transform sterile public gardens into miniature woodlands, roundabouts into rainforests, industrial estates into orchards, tidy verges into meadows. Let's ask, why aren't all farming methods earth-friendly as standard? Why don't all housing blueprints include the interests of wild plants and pollinators? How come most of the English countryside is forbidden to people, because of laws of trespass?

We need a new relationship with nature. A relationship built on empathy and reciprocity. This is a chance to create a new, biophilic society; a society in which connection with a healthy natural environment is a birthright; a society in which the destruction of nature is not a given.

RETHINKING OUR RESPONSIBILITY FOR OUR HEALTH

Plenty of people have responded to the coronavirus epidemic by observing that, when it comes to the nation's health, the phrase 'we're all in it together' is insultingly inaccurate. Few have championed a better, fitter future for all Britain's communities with more passion and energy than the sprinter and broadcaster Colin Jackson.

As Jackson notes, Covid-19 has been disproportionately felt by older people, poorer families and some ethnic minorities. This may be because of higher incidence of obesity or type 2 diabetes in parts of these communities. What is to be done? For Jackson, healthier habits start young. Radical ideas to increase exercise and improve diets for children at school can inculcate better lifestyles. Competitive sport is key.

I am very taken with his idea that we should treat the body as a luxury. I've never really considered that. But when you think about it, functioning kidneys, supple joints and arteries that aren't clogged up are just some of the greatest luxuries you could ever ask for. And, moreover, luxuries that not everyone has the good fortune to be born with. Yes, thinking – or rethinking – about it, treating our bodies as luxury goods to be nourished and treasured sounds like a plan for a healthier life after Covid-19.

The coronavirus pandemic has given us a once-in-a-lifetime opportunity to rethink the way that we look at our own health. Well, many of us may feel that we have overindulged on food and alcohol instead of doing exercise and eating healthier during lockdown. I, myself, struggled, so I quickly created some sort of fitness regime that was truly doable and sustainable, as none of us knew how long this pandemic was going to last. Maybe we think we're doing well by eating three a day of the government's recommended five-a-day fruit and veg, but it's not enough. We need the government and public health authorities, who have access to study information, to be honest about what it takes to live a balanced and healthy life, so we can take responsibility and choose.

At the moment, is the advice adequate? I feel not. It starts with the way we teach health and nutrition and exercise in schools. That itself is really important. The five a day should really be ten a day, but we must know, at a glance, what makes up that number of ten a day. Is it one banana, two pieces of broccoli? Hence the reason why good, early education is important. Of course we have the temptations of fast food, because it's there right in front of us. But we must learn how to enjoy it sensibly. Good education again here is so important: we need to treat our bodies like a luxury item that you can keep forever, not a fast-fashion purchase that you bin after a few weeks. We don't have to think about anything else apart from that. Because if we don't, underlying health problems like diabetes, heart disease, obesity, all of which make viruses such as Covid-19 much more effective killers, will be a problem.

There is talk at the moment that lockdown has the potential to create a lost generation of inactive youngsters – as they've missed schooling, they've also missed sport. So it's nice to actually hear that the government has announced that they're going to introduce health education into the curriculum, which will promote links between physical and mental health. Let's look at something like the Daily Mile, an initiative where pupils are encouraged to walk one mile a day, any time of the day that fits in with the working environment of teachers. Now, they're also giving very clear instructions to the pupil that it's not a race but it's a social activity. And research has already shown that mental and physical benefits have been gained from this. Something that is so simple can be truly powerful.

So, what is needed from here? Well, it is really important that health and wellbeing is truly prioritised in the school curriculum. It is important to know how we look both inside and out, and how we look after our bodies holistically. As I mentioned just now, all this is great for the general population, but we must also look very carefully at our national demographic. And what we find clearly is the BAME community are more likely to die from Covid, and suffer disproportionately with diabetes and prostate cancer, to name a few. But why? Maybe BAME health inequalities have suffered from a lack of research spending. Maybe because the community is relatively small in the overall population, meaning it's not worth the extra investment. Research, yes, has been done, telling us that we suffer more. But no answer has been given as to why. If you're part of this community, I feel it's really important to understand this. One epidemic, many tragedies. One opportunity for change, so let's take it.

MIRABELLE MORAH

RETHINKING OURSELVES

Did you know how just fast Africa – indeed, the world – is turning more Nigerian? The country's population is due to double by 2050. If that transpires, it will have over 400 million people, a bigger population than that of America. Human life is glorious, and many people will celebrate such growth. But it poses enormous challenges for that African power. They form the context for 19-year-old author Mirabelle Morah's essay.

She channels the inauguration speech of John F. Kennedy, in effect saying, 'Ask not what your country can do for you; ask what you can do for your country.' Except she goes further, in saying we should all ask ourselves what we can do for each other, regardless of national boundaries. I suspect her essay will chime with a sentiment you felt at various points over the long, hot, weird hibernation brought about by Covid-19. And that is a sense of reflection, of self-appraisal, wondering if this is the life you want to lead, or if you are doing as much good in the world as you really can. Morah's right, you know. We could all do better.

It's either I was too young to fully grasp the depth of this, or that I've been living in my own bubble for long, or maybe both and more. But honestly, not-so-good things have been happening since the start of 2020. I mean, is this the vision of 2020 of our dreams?

I honestly dislike giving life to negative thoughts but truly, all has not been well in Nigeria and around the globe. The world has always been bad, right? And maybe many of us didn't notice too much about the horrid existence others have been living in because we have been living in our own silos. But now? Since the pandemic hit it seems we've slightly woken up to the plights of others, thanks to the power of the media!

In our heads, hearts and mind, when Nigeria announced her first confirmed case of Covid-19 in March 2020, many of us thought to ourselves that, well, maybe the pandemic would finally force the government to look into the dilapidated state of our healthcare system in Nigeria and more funds would be pumped into our healthcare! Because if we have good health facilities in Nigeria, there would be fewer people travelling out of the country to seek better healthcare, and generally better healthcare systems improve the lives of the general populace, right? But as of June 2020, it was being reported over the news that the Nigerian federal government was proposing to slash the 2020 budgetary allocations for basic healthcare by about 43 per cent and also proposing to slash the country's basic education funds from circa N111.7 billion to N51.1 billion … I didn't even know how to feel! You can imagine my shock and upset. Amidst all this, Nigeria has also been going through various campaigns against rape and violence against women.

So will the world change for the better after Covid-19? You know what? I'm not going to ask myself that. Instead of looking at the world, saying '**the world**' and distancing myself from it, I'm rather asking myself now: Mirabelle, what are you currently doing to make yourself and the lives of others around you, better? Like Bryant McGill said: 'Change can be beautiful when we are brave enough to evolve with it, and change can be brutal when we fearfully resist.' There's a lot going on in the world right now and you can choose to be better for it or to be worse. But please don't choose the latter! And you don't have to wait for the post-Covid era to be better, to do better, to live a better life, or to treat others and the planet better. Why not choose **now**, as the best time to leave a positive legacy for future generations?

I've been conducting a survey via my initiative, Blank-Paperz Media, to see how the media can help our youths to be better, and we've launched Z'axis e-Magazine to remind young Africans that they're not alone in their change-making journeys. People have been donating to the causes they care about, organisations have been providing grants to others fighting against systemic racism and injustice. And you too can donate some clothing items to help those on the streets or do something kind.

I believe that if the world's going to be any better after Covid-19, aside from our governments, it'll take you and me to make this change. Because you and me? We live in this world and more often than not, we are the ones to select those who will represent us in the government. So, will the world change for the better after Covid-19? Well, will you change for the better after Covid-19?

NICCI GERRARD

RETHINKING
OLD AGE

This pandemic has had such sharply different effects on the old and young. For the young, it's mainly a source of economic rather than medical anxiety. For the old, and especially the very old, it has led to appalling sadness, loneliness and disconnection – even among those who didn't get the bug.

Nicci Gerrard writes bestselling novels with her husband Sean French, under the pseudonym Nicci French. The deeper, demographic context for her essay is inescapable: Europe, indeed, the West, has a very fast ageing population. This is a good thing: it's of course hugely welcome that people are living longer, and that the 100-year life is within reach for many more of us. But it does have massive, difficult implications for how we think of old people; and in particular, our duties towards them.

One of the most unbearable aspects of this pandemic – one that's very close to home for me – has been the enforced separation of grandparents and their grandchildren. There have been far too many awful stories of people in their seventies

*and eighties dying without the chance to say goodbye, whether
in person or at all. The least we owe it to them, as Gerrard so
beautifully put it, is to rethink the role, rights and needs of old
people in our time.*

When the tide goes out, we can see what's been there all along. And then – we can do something about what we see.

Often the first question we ask on hearing of a death is: how old were they? If they were young, that's heartbreaking. Middle-aged that's sad, for they died before their time. But if the answer is that they were old – and Covid-19 overwhelmingly kills the old – what then?

Often there's relief, sometimes even shrugging indifference: because they were running out of days, they would have died soon anyway. And because old people – above all those with dementia – tend to be invisible in a society that prizes youth, health, wealth, autonomy, individuality, purpose, power. And because they remind us – who are not yet old, or are in denial of our age – of our own decay and mortality. Old age and death is for other people. It's for them.

Over the past months, much energy, however botched, has gone on trying to get protective equipment and tests for hospitals. For a shocking length of time, this wasn't the case in care homes, and patients with the virus were – jaw-droppingly – even discharged there, as if care homes were dustbins. For weeks, deaths in hospitals were counted in the official toll, deaths in care homes were not. Didn't they count? For every life is precious, no life is disposable.

What's more, the government's so-called 'protective shield' around care homes that often failed to protect, meant that those in care homes have suffered anguish and in some cases fatal deterioration, as weeks turned into months and they were prevented from seeing those they loved and needed. Coronavirus is not the only thing we need to be alert to: radical loneliness and disconnection can kill (I speak as someone who's witnessed this in my own family, and I can tell you it's almost unbearable). It is excruciating to think of the suffering that's gone on: children calling to their parent through a fence, comforting them through a closed door. The helpless attempt at communication by phone, by Zoom. Last goodbyes by Skype. Death alone. These are the stories that should haunt us.

Every Thursday, the public cheered NHS frontline workers. Why didn't we also cheer those working day and night, scandalously underpaid and bewilderingly under-valued, in care homes where carnage was taking place in a system already in crisis; or for the unsung, underfunded family carers? Aren't they our heroes too? What topsy-turvy harsh society is it where those who tend to the most vulnerable have so little status and reward?

Now is the time to do things differently, do them better, and live united by common goals of decency and kindness. Empty platitudes and easy sorrow won't do. We have to put money, lots of money, and imagination, effort, love and hope, where they are most needed, and do to those who are in peril as we would be done by when our turn comes. And our turn will come – we are all vulnerable in the end, in this world we hold in common. If we are one of the lucky ones, old age is our future. Surely the future can be kinder than the past. And the future begins now.

BRIAN ENO

RETHINKING THE WINNERS

There are a lot of dichotomies knocking around to explain politics these days. Long gone is the boring old left versus right. Now we have open versus closed, Anywhere versus Somewhere, Leaveland versus Remainia ... I've even been known to mention Fast versus Slow in this context (see the introduction). For musician and producer Brian Eno, there's a better one. Life before, and during, this pandemic involves losers and winners.

In an unflinching assault on the cult of the strongman – those authoritarian leaders around the world who, though they've won elections, have little regard for most customs of democracy – Eno says that there is a better kind of leadership available to us.

His message is largely pessimistic: recent evidence bodes ill about our capacity to make the right choices. Like other essayists, he is right to ask: can it really be mere coincidence that so many of the democracies that have fared relatively well are led by women? And this despite the fact that the vast majority of national leaders in the world today, even among democracies, are men. Eno is also right, of course, to say that the weaknesses in international alliances exposed by this virus do not convey the impression of a world well placed to reduce, let alone reverse, the frying of Earth.

If we've learned one thing from the coronavirus experience it's that a certain style of government and leadership – a style that has dominated the last few years – isn't going to be of any use to us at all in the twenty-first century.

The countries that have suffered worst from Covid-19 all share a single governmental style: macho, media-savvy authoritarian leaders whose primary talent is self-promotion; who lie freely when it suits them; who disregard scientific advice if it doesn't enhance their own claims. These leaders gain power by manufacturing threats – Mexicans, immigrants, Muslims, Europeans, liberals, whatever you like – to create fake emergencies in which they can appear as saviours.

But in the face of an actual threat – coronavirus – all that macho posturing proves to be worse than useless. What was needed was preparation, expertise, cooperation and good data – all complete mysteries to the macho mind.

Contrast the performance of America, England and Brazil, at numbers one, two and three in the mortality charts at the time of writing (summer 2020) – with that of, say, Germany, New Zealand and Taiwan who've had much better results. All those three countries have female leaders, as do many of the other nations with better than average outcomes from Covid. The nations that have done well apparently spend more time listening to their scientists than to their ideologues, and don't consider evidence as a challenge to their manhood.

It's to their examples that we must look for a future.

Because we're running out of futures. By that I mean we're running out of choices about what kind of world we might inhabit. The urgency of climate change is propelling us towards two starkly contrasting visions. The first is the billionaires' utopia, where a few rich people secure themselves behind strong walls while the rest of us collapse in a fireball.

The other vision is our only chance: where we rethink our institutions and global arrangements so that in dealing with the upcoming disruptions of climate change and pandemics we build something new – something better than we have now. This sounds idealistic but in fact it's the only option. We have to make a society that works in the long term by valuing all its different intelligences; by engaging everybody rather than excluding most. It's a future built on cooperation and inclusion, not division. We've seen the first green shoots of it in the better responses to Covid, and in the proliferation of anti-discrimination activism (which could also be called pro-inclusion activism).

If we want to live in a stable, creative society we need to rethink things so that everybody in it feels welcomed and valued. The more people have an investment in society the more they will want to nurture and improve it.

This isn't about the winners being generous enough to share a bit of their spoils with the losers. It's about realising that a world with a few winners and a lot of losers isn't a tenable world.

JUDE BROWNE
RETHINKING RESPONSIBILITY

The cultural turn in our politics, from a socio-economic axis (class) to a socio-cultural one (identity), has various roots, including demographic churn and multiculturalism. The intellectual demands it places on us are only just becoming clear.

Identity politics is a loose term, but it generally asserts the paramount importance of group membership. If you belong to a group, you get certain rights. As the prevalence of group identity has grown, there has been inflation in rights. But the flip-side of any right is a duty – to uphold that right. My right is your duty; and vice versa.

The inflation in rights has generated inflation in duties, but we don't talk about that nearly as much as we ought to. Nearly three decades after David Selbourne's The Principle of Duty, *politicians recoil from that word, thinking it anachronistic. It often gets translated to responsibility; yet something precious is lost in translation. Societies as diverse, divided and digital as ours need, urgently, to revive a deeper and nobler idea of responsibility.*

The eminent Professor Jude Browne makes the case for doing just that exquisitely here. As she says, the pandemic has challenged us to think much harder not just about what we owe each other, but why. As she puts it, in a lovely phrase, the question of how we contribute to 'the background conditions of each other's prospects' requires better answers.

I wrote in the introduction that western societies are experiencing a crisis of connection. Browne chronicles the malaise – and endorses a solution.

Witnessing the spread of Covid-19 across the globe has shown us just how connected we humans really are, even when some of our political choices seem to be saying something very different. Covid-19 makes us rethink responsibility. What does it mean to be responsible? Who is responsible and for what?

Blame is a powerful political tool and it is certainly important to identify who is responsible for failures, wrongs and injustices of the past. But there is another sort of responsibility: a shared responsibility that looks forward as well as back and is grounded in the connectedness of humanity, in that we all are contributing to the background conditions of each other's prospects. This sort of connection is what we call structural and can produce profound harms that result not from maliciousness, wrong-doing or failures that we can readily trace back to culprits, but rather the amorphous, accumulated, unintended outcomes of masses of ordinary individuals, groups and institutions, going about their everyday activities. These structural dynamics require a different sort of responsibility grounded in the very connectedness that we have been reminded of in this pandemic – this sort of responsibility is based on the contributions we unwittingly make to the background conditions of these structural harms, not just in our own towns and cities but across national borders.

We have seen the immense power of social movements, such as #MeToo, which emboldened many women by illustrating just how many others shared their experience of sexual abuse and harassment; Black Lives Matter protesting against racial violence and discrimination; or individuals such as Greta Thunberg, whose activism has convinced so many that we ought to pull the emergency brake on climate change. But how do we put structural responsibility into our political frameworks and the sorts of state apparatus that we have at our disposal with the macro-level coordinating power we need?

Politicians, officials and experts, important though they are in our democracy, forge perspectives that are necessarily shaped by their professional position. Politicians, in particular, always have their eye on the next election, which tends to keep their interest focused on the shorter term. Covid-19 has reminded us that we need to listen to the experts, but that they are not always in touch with the concerns of the public, or listened to by the politicians. What we don't have is enough public engagement with the pluralistic details, the science and the evidence, so that a longer-term public interest can start to dominate politics.

Recently, however, we have started to experiment with new forms of politics.

Imagine receiving an invitation, along with 99 other randomly selected members of society (much like jury duty, you are chosen by social category, such as gender, age, ethnicity, place of residence etc). Your responsibility is to deliberate competing evidence presented by respected experts with sometimes diametrically different views, submissions from other members of the public, interest groups, social movements and a wide range of public and private institutions and industry. You are watched and listened to by the public you represent, and together you go on an exploratory journey to decide on what we ought to do, not in the shorter-termist mode in which our politicians tend to operate, not according to the private interests of industry or the market but rather with a view to forging a long-term collective public interest. These particular deliberative conditions are *not* to be found in the everyday and they are a very different form of public engagement with evidence than that to be found in the echo-chambers of Twitter or Facebook. They are, rather, those of a citizens' assembly.

Rather than only sitting outside of our political structures, I'd like to see elements of citizens' assemblies built into them, our regulators and our public bodies – taking the experts with them but focusing on our responsibilities not only to each other but to future generations – and requiring that our politicians do the same.

Elif Shafak

RETHINKING UNCERTAINTY

Pandemics unite the world in fear. That the pathogen among us is invisible and yet everywhere adds to the pervasive uncertainty we all feel. Will we be next? Are my parents vulnerable? Am I safe? These fears are legitimate and cannot easily be suppressed. Nor should they be. Yet there are softer fears, or anxieties, which we all of us navigate every day. In Elif Shafak's reckoning, embracing them as part of the warp and weft of our lives is much healthier than wishing them away.

This prolific cosmopolitan writer, with Turkish ancestry, has developed a strong line in homespun wisdom in recent years. In many of her public utterances Shafak celebrates the insight of poets and philosophers through the ages. And uncertainty, or doubt, is one of those subjects that has attracted more attention than most.

Yeats' verdict in 'The Second Coming' – 'the best lack all conviction, while the worst are full of passionate intensity' – is familiar. Less so is Auden's assertion in his commonplace book: 'We must believe before we can doubt, and doubt before we can deny.' And, half a century earlier, Bertrand Russell wrote: 'One of the painful things about our time is that those who feel certainty are stupid, and those with any imagination and understanding are filled with doubt and indecision.'

It was a rare misstep for dear old Bertrand: what he says is true of all eras, and not just his. As Shafak and each of those thinkers suggest, certainty is the first refuge of the scoundrel, and doubt the beginning of wisdom. If the pandemic prompts more of us to feel comfortable with the latter, some good will have come of it.

It always starts with words. The manifestation of both what's best and what's worst in us human beings. The darkest chapters in history did not begin with concentration camps and gas chambers or systemic discrimination and racial violence. All of that came later. What preceded were the subtle shifts in daily language, the choice of terms used for people deemed to be different, and the derogatory meanings attributed to them. Equally, though, during times of positive change and social transformation, once again, words were the precursors of progress.

For the past two years now there is one word that has appeared, over and over, in all search engines across the world. A quite simple one, at first glance: 'Why?'

This seemingly ordinary monosyllable has been repeated on so many occasions that recently Google Trends made a video explaining that ours has been a time of 'deep questioning, as the world searched "why" more than ever'. The why-questions raised by citizens everywhere varied greatly from personal to collective, from national to international: 'Why can't I sleep?', 'Why do I struggle with anxiety?', 'Why do I feel angry/frustrated/emotionally worn out?', 'Why are people protesting?', 'Why do we need more empathy?' ... and so on. The same video also argued that, 'In times of uncertainty, people seek understanding and meaning'. Therefore there is a direct correlation between the sudden proliferation of why-questions in our lives and the characteristic unpredictability of the age we find ourselves in.

Uncertainty has become a trademark of our times. But how we respond to uncertainty needs radical rethinking.

Years ago, when I used to live in Istanbul, I was interviewed by an American scholar who was doing research on 'women writers in the Middle East'. At some point in our conversation the academic told me that it was 'very understandable' for me to be a feminist since I lived in Turkey and this was obviously a patriarchal country. I realised in surprise that she did not seem to find the struggle for women's rights as necessary for the land where she came from, since the USA, and the West in general, were historically 'beyond such worries'.

It was a dualistic view that separated the world into two parts: on the one hand were 'liquid lands' where one had to fight for equality, inclusion, human rights, freedom of speech and democracy. On the other hand were 'solid lands' where such struggles had already been completed, progress long-achieved, rights duly earned. Feminism, therefore, was needed in liquid lands, but not so much in solid lands, where gender equality was no longer a problem.

Ever since 2016, this binary interpretation of the world has been shattered to pieces. Having seen the rise of populist movements everywhere, and witnessed the multiple threats against liberal pluralistic democracies, the backlash against women's rights and LGBT+ rights and the loss of freedom of speech, we now understand better that there is no such thing as 'solid lands versus liquid lands' and, in fact, we are all living through liquid times.

History does not always move in a linear progressive direction. Democracy is much more fragile than we initially assumed – a delicate ecosystem of checks and balances. For a democracy to survive we need more than the ballot box. We have entered an era in which we all need to become active, involved citizens, East and West.

If the abrupt changes in politics deepened our sense of uncertainty worldwide, coronavirus undoubtedly made things worse. The pandemic did not create as much as reveal the existing fractures and inequalities in our societies. It also proved that we are all interconnected. You can erect walls around a nation or a community or a region or a tribe, but you cannot shut the rest of the world completely outside. Being interconnected increases our perception of uncertainty but it also offers new probabilities as to the solutions we can find together to our problems as humanity.

None of this is to deny the fact that uncertainty can be extremely tiring, stressful. It aggravates our levels of anxiety, confusion, even a sense of helplessness. And fear too.

Fear itself is a corrosive force, one that produces a deep longing for simplicity, safety, homogeneity. Yet this can constitute a dangerous moment because demagogues understand the expectation and seize the opportunity to further their own interests. They walk onto the political stage promising not only safety and sameness, but also an engineered certainty.

It is a false promise, though, a mere illusion. In a world as complex, interconnected and ambiguous as ours, it is wiser and healthier to acknowledge uncertainty as an essential part of life rather than try to suppress or erase it by following populist demagogues. The 'easy shortcut' to simplicity that they try to sell us only serves to trigger a yearning to go back to a mythical time in history, a romantic golden age that never was.

When we struggle with uncertainty, and we all do from time to time, it's worth remembering that if there is one thing that is scarier than confusion it is the total lack of it. The complete eradication of doubt. The ascendancy of dogmas. The moment we stop questioning our own truths is the moment we stop learning. Absolute convictions and rigid certainties have done far more damage in this world than any potential uncertainty ever could.

At the end of the day, uncertainty is a closed box we are scared to open. But when we do, we realise it was a music box, and dancing inside to an unknown melody is the most unlikely couple: Faith and Doubt. Optimism and Pessimism. Hope and Melancholy. Change and Tradition. Story and Silence.

Open the box. Listen to the melody. So long as they are dancing, they are also transforming each other. So long as they are dancing, they are also offering a potential for the better.

HOW
WE
LIVE

AMANDA LEVETE

RETHINKING HOW WE LIVE

Amanda Levete is unquestionably one of the most influential and impactful architects alive today. Her revolutionary approach to the built environment has always tried to reconcile technology with nature. That is her ambition here, too.

In recent years there has been a revival of classical approaches to architecture and public space. A consensus may be emerging that modern architecture, of the kind Le Corbusier and his followers championed, hasn't always been loved by the public. Levete evokes an alternative kind of public architecture, which prioritises wellbeing over efficiency, and belonging over utility.

I am very struck by her view that architecture reflects the social conditions from which it springs. It follows that an architecture by the people and for the people can only arise if 'the people' realise how important their public spaces are. It is certainly true that, as we re-evaluate the form, function and, above all, feel of our cities, architecture that pleases the eye and satisfies the soul ought to be in much greater demand

than the utilitarian horrors that have, as Levete eloquently
argues, so blighted urban landscapes in the past few decades.

We cannot unknow what has happened, we cannot ignore the risks our future holds and we cannot go back to normal without reflecting deeply. This pandemic has raised overwhelming existential issues: issues around race, inequality and the environment. But it's also revealed the breathtaking power of collective responsibility and shown that radical change is possible. With offices working from home, each of us has established our own rhythm to suit our personality and circumstances. It has brought a new balance to our lives and given us more control over our working day, and it's going to be hard to give that up. As much as I miss the spontaneity and joy of face-to-face contact with my team, our remoteness has led to a heightened sense of collaboration. Adversity has reminded us that we all have a part to play in our interconnected world. To be more responsible, accountable and generous. And to appreciate the importance of small things: searching out that corner of sunlight on the front steps and chatting to passers-by.

Lockdown has thrown into sharp relief the hardship of those who do not have the luxury of generous indoor space or access to a garden. We have got to rethink this imbalance. Space and nature are a need; they are not a luxury. But need alone will not lead to change: desire will. We need to desire a more equitable society and then design a more equitable model around that, to create places where we can live better together and live better with nature. Places that promote a network of cooperation, where people can rediscover the art of living and where wellbeing, not efficiency, is the measure of success.

Historically, buildings and cities have been shaped by pandemics. At an urban scale, the 1870s cholera outbreak in London led to the creation of the sewage system, wider streets and the Victoria Embankment, a road and river-walk along the Thames. On a more domestic scale, houses in sixteenth-century Spain were painted with lime, because its antibacterial properties helped prevent the spread of the plague. It's a lovely example of need evolving into the vernacular. And although the science wasn't fully understood at the time, it was one of the first examples of nanotechnology in action.

Nanotechnology inspired a research project we embarked on pre-Covid, a collaboration with a professor of biological physics at the University of Oxford. It feels particularly relevant now with the new focus on science. In times of crisis, there's a tendency to retreat into the comfort of what we know. But we must resist this and continue to dream. With this project, we're rethinking how to use nature's strategies in trees to grow the materials of the future. By extracting the lignin from wood, manipulating the cellulose structure and infusing bio-resins, we aim to take the research out of the lab to make a new material that is stronger than steel, a better insulator than glass and that lets the light in. It will be, in effect, transparent wood. If we can reconcile nature and technology, we can find new ways to build that are positive for our environment. And by reconciling responsibility and freedom without contradiction, we can design new models for living. Opportunities to effect radical change are rare, so we have to act now and we have to make sure we remember.

RETHINKING PROGRESS

As a historian, Ferguson has always drawn on two other disciplines. First, economics, his specialism. Second, biology, specifically Darwinism. In this powerful essay, Ferguson, a prolific analyst of the deep global trends reshaping our world, marries the two.

In wondering how historians will look back on Covid-19, Ferguson relates a fable of the weak and the strong. Nietzsche inevitably rears his sore head. The strong are strong enough to survive these indiscriminate pathogens, because they adapt well. And the weak were going to die anyway. He's not talking about people here, but varieties of institution; and in his portrait of some bureaucracies, universities and media, Ferguson will leave you in no doubt of who he would like the institutional victims of Covid-19 to be. Whether his wishes are fulfilled will, alas, be left to later historians to say.

I must say I was not surprised to read his implied view that any intergenerational conflict, if it transpires, will *have roots other than Covid-19. Ferguson's long view of the present crisis puts it in its proper context, and gives weight to his predictions.*

Pandemics, like world wars and global financial crises, are history's great interruptions. Whether manmade or naturally occurring, whether anticipated or bolts from the blue, they're also moments of revelation. It isn't just that a catastrophe divides us all up into three groups: the prematurely dead (always a minority of our species even in the worst disasters such as the Black Death or the Second World War), the lucky survivors and the permanently wounded or traumatised. The catastrophe also separates the fragile from the resilient and the antifragile, Nassim Taleb's wonderful word to describe something that actually becomes stronger under stress. (Remember Nietzsche: what doesn't kill me makes me stronger.) Some cities, corporations, states and empires collapse under the force of the shock; others survive. But a third category emerges stronger from the crisis. I'd hazard a guess that the United States is in category two, not one. The People's Republic of China may turn out to be in category one, not two. The Republic of China, Taiwan, is in category three.

So let's think about Covid-19 within this framework. By the standards of past pandemics, it is not one of history's worst. It currently ranks around 22nd in terms of the global mortality rate. Then again, there's much that we don't yet fully understand about this virus. It seems now that, with a regime of mass testing, contact tracing and targeted quarantining, a country can drive this virus to extinction, as it relies heavily on so-called super-spreaders for its transmission and disproportionately sickens or kills people in older age groups. Unlike the First World War, this pandemic really could have been all over by Christmas, if we'd been smart. With the advent of efficacious vaccines, it should largely be over by summer 2021. Similarly, there's a good chance that our economies can snap back into life once this becomes clear. Then again, there's a much worse scenario in which we spend years playing whack-a-mole with SARS-CoV-2 with no immunity that really lasts. Perhaps the virus really doesn't harm the young or perhaps it does in ways we haven't yet understood. So much is still uncertain.

We don't even know for sure what the political and geopolitical consequences of the pandemic will be. Does the populist right ultimately win because the vital importance of national borders is no longer in doubt? Or does the left make the case for even bigger government, in the wake of big government's very evident failure in the US and the UK? How lasting will the impact be of the protests that followed the killing of George Floyd in Minneapolis? Does this common enemy reduce international tensions, or does 'Cold War II' between China and the United States intensify? Does it even turn into a hot war over Taiwan? We can't yet know.

Three things I believe can be said now with some confidence. First, Covid-19 is to social life what AIDS was to sexual life. It'll change our behaviour but by no means enough to avert a significant number of premature deaths. I personally welcome a new age of social distancing, but then I'm a natural misanthrope who hates crowds and parties. I really don't care if I never get on another plane or never see New York again. Most people, however, will be unable to resist the temptations of post-lockdown gregariousness. There'll be unsafe socialising, just as there's still unsafe sex, even after more than three decades and 30 million deaths from HIV/AIDS.

Second, and for that reason, most big cities aren't over. Do we all now vacate the Great Wen for the country, there to cultivate our vegetable gardens in splendid rustic isolation? Probably not. It takes a lot to kill a city. True, just over a century after Thomas Mann wrote *Death in Venice*, Venice is pretty much dead. But it wasn't cholera that killed it – try the shifting pattern of international trade – just as Covid-19 won't kill London and New York. It'll just make them cheaper and grungier.

Finally, let's reflect on the pandemic's impact on generational imbalances that had grown intolerable in many societies in recent years. Has Covid-19 been sent by Freya, the Goddess of Youth, to emancipate Millennials and Generation Z from carrying the fiscal burden of an excessive number of elderly people? It's tempting to marvel at this ageist virus. No previous pandemic was so discriminating against the elderly and in favour of the young. In truth, however, the impact of Covid-19 in terms of excess mortality will probably not be great enough to make much difference. In the short run, the majority of old people will remain retired, relatively few will die prematurely – hardly any in some countries, notably in Japan. The young, meanwhile, will be the ones struggling to find jobs, other than with Amazon. Plagues don't halt progress if progress is happening. The same London that suffered the last great bubonic plague outbreak of 1665 was about to become the central hub of an extraordinary commercial empire, a humming hive of scientific and financial innovation. No pathogen could stop that.

Our plague is likely to have the biggest impacts on places where progress had stopped and stagnation had set in. First in line, I hope, will be the bureaucracies that, in some countries, including Britain and America, so badly failed to deal with this crisis. Next, I hope, will be those universities that were more interested in propagating woke ideology than teaching all that can be profitably learned from the human past. Finally, may the pandemic clear out those media institutions that insisted on covering it as if it were all a function of the foibles of a few presidents, prime ministers and advisors. If stagnating institutions are shaken up by this disaster, there's just a chance that we'll see a return to progress in places where, up until 2020, the most striking trend had been degeneration. By killing those parts of our system that failed this test, Covid-19 might just make us stronger.

DAVID WALLACE-WELLS

RETHINKING CONSENSUS

David Wallace-Wells's book The Uninhabitable Earth, *which warned about the imminent and likely effects of climate change, was frequently described as apocalyptic. The trouble with that analysis is that the apocalypse isn't real, whereas ecological devastation already is. So his upbeat tone in this essay may surprise you.*

As Wallace-Wells notes, fear is one of the great drivers of human history. Fear has driven much of the response to this pandemic, both global and personal. As a result, it has dragged previously unthinkable ideas from the fringes of political debate to the centre. Wallace-Wells finds hope in the adoption, by Joe Biden, of activist policies on health and the environment. He has gone, as Wallace-Wells notes, from being seen as the face of the establishment to just about the most radical Democrat nominee for a century. There is an irony at play in this essay, because just as Wallace-Wells celebrates Biden's evolution, he talks of an epochal shift and the creation of a new political generation. That it should be, in effect, led by a 78-year-old

who entered the Senate in 1973 is emblematic of the kind of
strange occurrence that attends the death of any consensus, and
the shift between epochs that is this book's theme.

I'm not really much of a utopianist, having spent a lot of the last few years thinking about the prospects for quite punishing levels of climate change. Within the first few weeks of the coronavirus pandemic, I felt myself actually doing a lot of looking on the bright side. The entire northern hemisphere was bunkered into shelter-in-place lockdowns, all out of concern for our health and the health of those around us. Amazingly, those policies were improvised, nation by nation, and sometimes community by community. As were best practices around social distancing, mask wearing and all the rest. We actually learned from each other and a whole global public health programme sprang up, uncoordinated, in the space of a month or so. Fear is an incredible motivator.

If you're on the left, especially, you probably read a number of essays then suggesting we should spend our time in quarantine considering what kind of society we really wanted to build and live in. That idea seemed pretty naïve to me but in the US, of all places, we've somehow managed to do it. There are now unprecedented nationwide protests against police brutality and systemic racism and unprecedented public support for those causes. To stabilise the economy, the government has already spent four times what it did in the aftermath of the great recession and will likely spend more. Economists who worried then about deficits have been almost universally radicalised. Not just vanguard figures like Stephanie Kelton and Mariana Mazzucato but people in institutions at the very centre of the economic establishment: Paul Romer, the IMF, *The Economist* and the *FT*.

This isn't just the work of the pandemic, though the crisis has accelerated things. It's also taught us in ways climate change hasn't yet managed. That we all live within nature, however much we feel superior to and protected against it. It's taught us that early action in response to a threat is invariably preferable. It's taught us that we can't starve state services of funding and support and expect them to function. And it's taught us, in the US in particular, where really we should be embarrassed as a country to not have learned it before, that on matters of public health especially, the neoliberal answer was not sufficient. It cannot go it alone.

For all of these reasons and all of these ways, it seems possible that rather than having our political spirits broken by Covid-19, we are, in fact, passing rapidly through an epochal political shift to a new political generation, divided from the last sclerotic one by this disease and the disorienting suffering it has caused.

Here in the US, activist energy and the leftward movement of the middle have already pulled Joe Biden so much that the man who, six months ago, was the very face of status-quo politics, is now the most radical Democratic nominee for president in almost a century. A month ago, his climate policy was the most expansive and expensive ever put forward by a nominee. Now, a panel of the Democratic National Committee wants him to expand it as much as sixfold.

Somehow, as the pandemic killed many of us, and terrified the rest of us, it may have begun a generational political transformation too. We needed that, because in the old system, 100,000 Americans and 50,000 Brits have (so far) died of public indifference. Those numbers should be unconscionable, if we allow our moral antennae to actually be tuned to the suffering, rather than tuning it out, an act of reflective, grotesque normalisation. Those numbers are also tiny compared to the suffering that is possible, given unchecked global warming. Which means, perhaps more than anything else, more even than decarbonising, we also have to try to learn to stop normalising, beginning with how we regard the spread of this pandemic now into the global south. Here's hoping and to looking on the bright side.

Margaret MacMillan

RETHINKING INTERNATIONAL COOPERATION

From climate change to infectious disease, our inter-dependence is essential to our condition. And yet at the same time, as Samantha Power argues in a similar essay (see page 111), the multilateral institutions that came out of the Second World War – and particularly Bretton Woods in 1944 – are under the greatest strain since their founding.

As historian Margaret MacMillan makes clear, the spirit of collective endeavour that has allowed the world to make such progress against so many ills has been 'painful' work. It involves trade-offs, sacrifices and disappointments. International cooperation is hard won and easily lost; and whether Covid-19 leads to more or less of it depends largely on the conviction, and calibre, of leaders in our time. On this score, it is notable that several of the countries that are widely thought to have dealt effectively with the pandemic – Taiwan, New Zealand, Germany – have female leaders; and many of those who are widely

considered to have been ineffective – Brazil, America – have
strongman leaders.

Authoritarian populism has been, if not in the ascendant,
certainly on the rise in recent years. The leaders of such regimes
tend not to be champions of international cooperation. This,
as MacMillan explains, bodes ill.

Maps and charts can show flight paths, the internet, shipping routes, the flows of money, commodities and goods but that is only a part of the global web that joins us. With rapid communications, family ties among people, often on different continents, we are aware of each other as never before. For better or worse, we live in a global society.

We have come to understand that what happens in one part of the world can ripple outwards. Locusts in Africa affect crops destined for the global north, fires in the Amazon or Indonesia change weather on the other side of the planet, civil wars push millions of refugees to new countries and continents.

Great catastrophes can make us resolve to change. After the Second World War, nations came together to create the United Nations and the Bretton Woods trio of the World Bank, the International Monetary Fund and the World Trade Organization and to lay the foundations of the European Union so that we would not repeat the mistakes of the 1930s. The world is far from perfect but those institutions have made a real difference.

Many of us continue to hope, as they did after 1945, that our world will become still better – fairer, more stable and peaceful. We have a multiplicity of organisations, official and non-official, to manage our interconnected world, from the World Health Organization to the International Committee of the Red Cross. We have accepted responsibility for each other through humanitarian aid, UN peacekeeping, or disaster relief. In that dense web that joins us are darker threads: crime, conspiracy theories, cruel ideologies, or cyber mischief-making. But we can deal with those if we work together.

The Covid-19 pandemic has shown us just how interdependent we are – and how vulnerable. Viruses jump suddenly from other creatures to humans and do not respect borders any more than the birds or animals or fleeing humans that can carry them. Yet we have not always responded wisely. Countries have hoarded information – China took too long to alert the rest of the world to Covid-19 – as well as equipment and drugs. Too often, irresponsible leaders – and ordinary citizens too – have lashed out with unfounded accusations: that the virus was a deliberate act of biological warfare or carried by minorities. The World Health Organization can certainly be criticised but we need such a body that can coordinate a global response to a global crisis. So for the United

States to pull out [in July 2020] is a grievous blow to the international order.

That order was already under attack, from reckless states such as Putin's Russia, a United States under President Trump withdrawing from leadership, renouncing international agreements and straining long-standing alliances and an increasing number of authoritarian and often demagogic leaders. The temptation is there, as it was in the 1930s, for peoples to turn inwards, put up barriers and walls, and shrug our shoulders at the world and its many problems. That would be, as it was then, very costly folly.

The present crisis and ones to come won't leave us alone, whatever we wish. We may not have much time left before the next one, whether a pandemic or a severe depression, even social and political collapse in vulnerable countries. And looming over all those is the still greater threat of climate change which is pushing our planet and the human race to their limits. We must not lose the sense we have gained so painfully that we inhabit the same world, and we must not forget the fear and sense of urgency with which we mobilised ourselves to deal with Covid-19. We are going to need them.

RETHINKING NATURE

One idea, one notion, one principle, simple but overwhelmingly strong, has sustained and cohered all of Prince Charles's interventions in debates about the environment throughout his life. That is the feeling that we should live in harmony with the Earth. Humankind cannot think of itself as unbound; we are part of, and limited by, the natural world. He elaborates on the practicalities of this in the powerful, urgent essay you are about to read, in which he asks us to rethink nature.

The principle from which he begins is, by his own frequent admission, a complex and contested one. Of course we sapiens are a late, perhaps final, chapter in the beautiful saga of Darwinism. Of course we are humbled by tornados and tsunamis, volcanoes and viruses. But we are also the animal that became a god. In the state of nature that some – though not all – in the green movement romanticise, we might still have a life expectancy in the forties, endure disease without medicine and struggle to imagine the engineering miracles of television or the smartphone. Our intervention in natural processes makes us human. And yet of course, excessive intervention can cause devastation. A happier, healthier balance – harmony, if you like – is not just good for the soul, but vital for the preservation of this precious marble of which each of us is but a brief custodian. In highlighting the excesses of our interventions, and the degrading of nature that has characterised so much otherwise admirable human development, the future King is here nothing less than a green revolutionary.

Even if one disputes his recommendations, nobody could dispute the facts that he has mobilised here to fuel them. To live in an age when biodiversity is declining as never before, and a million species seem on the brink of vanishing forever from the Earth, is to confront a historical moment of tremendous peril. It is humanity's unique blessing to be both a part of nature and apart from it. But if there is one aspect of our lives that needs rethinking, surely it is how we all flourish on Earth without frying it.

As we rethink our world in the wake of the pandemic, it is increasingly clear that the health and wellbeing of people and planet are inextricably linked. To restore harmony, we must put nature at the centre of our economy. This is often described as the circular bio-economy.

From Africa to Latin America, there are a number of excellent examples of the national and regional commitments that could be transformed through this approach. Yet to succeed, I believe the following actions are needed.

We need to restore biodiversity, and we need to use nature to drive prosperity for all.

Biodiversity is declining faster than at any time in human history. And nearly a million species are currently at risk of extinction. Which means we are making ourselves ever more vulnerable to future pandemics.

Natural resources like agriculture, landscapes and forests are owned by a wide range of small to large stakeholders. Better valuing these resources offers an opportunity to generate a more equitable distribution of income, jobs and prosperity. So we need to rethink land, food and health systems.

Regenerative agriculture can enable agriculture to become a net carbon sink by restoring soil fertility. It can also address climate change, increase prosperity, revitalise rural communities and enhance human health.

Regenerative agriculture nourishes the soil on which all life depends, especially the microbial life that sequesters carbon in the earth.

It implies a significant shift from industrial farming towards mosaics of sustainable regenerative production systems, based on smallholder organic farming. Because more people are needed to do the work, regenerative farming increases employment, helping meet the demand for jobs.

To empower nature, we need to invest in her, particularly in reforestation. Recent discoveries have revealed the essential role of forests for the global water cycle and food security. The virtues of restoring tree cover for soil and water conservation are nowhere better illustrated than in a heavily deforested country like Ethiopia. With a pledge to restore 15 million hectares of forest, and with the help of water conservation techniques such as terraces, the regrowing trees increase the water infiltration and help springs re-emerge, which reduces the walking distance to water sources, and opens opportunities for irrigated horticulture and improved nutrition.

Every year, nearly 3 million hectares of forest are lost in Africa, and yet Africa is unique in that it has the largest restoration opportunity of any continent in the world, with more than 700 million hectares of deforested land.

In this regard, a real opportunity to transform the environment, and millions of lives and livelihoods, exists in the form of the African Forest Landscape Restoration Initiative. This is a country-led effort to restore 100 million hectares of deforested and degraded landscapes across Africa. The same kind of ambition exists in South America in the form of the 2020 Initiative.

There are opportunities, therefore, to scale up restoration in ways that generate multiple benefits for local communities. These opportunities can be realised if concerted action is mobilised to generate the immense added value that species-rich forests can provide – specifically in restored and resilient landscapes, improved soil fertility, enhanced agricultural productivity and food security, reduced desertification, improved water resources, increased biodiversity and green jobs.

Therefore, with so much opportunity in front of us, let us rethink our relationship with nature and reset for a better future. We have absolutely no time to waste.

Onora O'Neill

RETHINKING DIGITAL POWER

Can democracy survive Facebook? In a better world, we might
have asked can Facebook survive democracy? As the BBC's first
media editor, my main job is reporting on the friction between
democracy and technology. The data kings of California are
undoubtedly a profound challenge to both democracy and
capitalism in our age. Yet so intense is their lobbying effort,
and so distracted or disjointed have democracies been in their
regulatory response, that these tech giants have done irrevers-
ible damage to our public domain.

The truth is, Facebook and other social giants are both the
most democratic and the most anti-democratic tools ever invented.
They give the previously powerless a voice, spread information
instantly across the globe, and generate communities. But they
also allow anonymous and unaccountable forces to influence elec-
tions, and lies to go to viral. Some day, we will realise how bizarre
it was to allow them such power with so little accountability.

It was back in 2002 that Baroness O'Neill's Reith Lecture,
called 'A Question of Trust', examined how that precious

commodity had been eroded in our public life. It's remarkable to think Facebook hadn't even been founded then. Like all social goods, trust is easily destroyed but not easily created. The same is true of democracy.

There's little disagreement in the United Kingdom that the post-pandemic world will need environmentally sustainable policies. Since sustainability in one country's not enough, no local or regional consensus will be enough to ensure that we get there. As many already realise, it will be grindingly hard to stem global warming. However, we not only need a future of survivable carbon levels but one with sustainable political structures and this too will be very hard to achieve and maintain. After the fall of the Berlin Wall, many hoped for a more stable and democratic future. More recently, enthusiasts imagined that digital technologies would ensure the spread of democracy. This happy illusion has now been dispelled. It is evident that digital technologies without the right surrounding legislation and structures can damage, as well as support, both democracy and good governance.

For democracy to work, citizens must be able to communicate their views and to follow and assess others' views. They need to be listeners as well as speakers, readers as well as writers. They must engage and communicate with those whose views they do not share. And they must seek to judge which claims are worth attention and which are flaky or false, or indeed fake. Digital technologies provide unsurpassed ways of distributing content, but they can be used to damage rather than support accurate and disciplined communication and critical engagement. They can be used to undermine others' standing and their claims and to further the agendas of those who market, control and purchase online influence. They can be used without regard to the ethical and epistemic standards that matter for communication and for democracy. And they may undermine or suppress certain views and isolate or undermine those who hold them.

These realities are increasingly recognised but many currently proposed remedies are woefully inadequate. It's not enough to introduce more fact-checking or to improve digital literacy. It's not enough to address the so-called online harms that certain uses of social media inflict. Rather we need to address the power structures that provide a cloak of anonymity for those who purchase and market opportunities to influence public life. Pre-digital democracies have regulated party-political expenditure and conduct, but in the digital world influence can be wielded anonymously by those who control and purchase the targeting of online content. They need not be citizens of the countries whose voters they seek to influence and their electioneering expenditure need not be declared. If we want to restore and protect democracy, we shall need to address the realities of power in the digital world.

MATTHEW WALKER

RETHINKING SLEEP

Let me pitch a wonder drug to you. This magic pill will radically improve your memory, metabolism and immune system. After taking it, you'll absorb new information faster, feel less tired and anxious, and be much, much less likely to suffer heart disease. This pill has almost no side effects. It's free. Would you take it? Something like this irresistible idea formed the core of Matthew Walker's bestselling book, Why We Sleep.

In America alone, according to a 2016 study, sleep deprivation cost the country $400 billion and 1.23 million lost days of work annually. Many people wrongly assume sleeping less is good for productivity. In fact, as Walker argues, the opposite is true. Sleep is an economic and public health crisis.

Perhaps a new, better attitude to sleep in the post-pandemic world, where we stop staring at gleaming screens before going to bed even more exhausted and wired than we already were, is the revolution we need. I hadn't realised how strong the connection between sleep and our immune system is. Given we've been trying, collectively, to fight off a virus, perhaps we might start to think of a good night's sleep as a way of being kind not just to ourselves – but to each other.

Our sleep does seem to have changed during the pandemic. An early report from a sleep-tracking company involving over 60,000 people reported that total sleep time had initially increased by 20 per cent.

Two more recent studies suggest it is more nuanced and less extreme than this headline figure. One study showed that, on average, total sleep time had increased by 15 minutes, but people's sense of the quality of their sleep had decreased. A second study reported that, in general, people had increased their sleep by 30 minutes during the weekdays, and even added 24 minutes at the weekend.

However, it is very clear that there is a non-trivial sub-set of people for whom sleep has become much more difficult during the pandemic, not reflected in the grand average values of these studies. It's not a one-size-fits-all outcome.

More consistent is the fact that people are starting to sleep more in harmony with what we call our chronotype. In other words, are you an evening person, a morning person, or are you somewhere in between? Keep in mind that you don't really get a choice in picking your chronotype. It's largely genetically determined, so it's hardwired. It's not your 'fault' if you are an evening type.

With the pandemic removing the need for commuting and getting kids to school for many people, schedules have become more flexible. This is especially helpful to the evening types. They can go to bed later, when their internal biological clock actually wants them to sleep, and wake up a little later, just as they have been genetically hardwired to do. As a result, it's almost a case of revenge of the evening night owls during the pandemic.

But what does this mean for the future in terms of sleep? Well, perhaps when people return to work, what if we asked everyone to fill out a very brief set of questions about their preferred sleep times? When would they prefer to wake up? When would they prefer to go to bed? And companies could then start to try and accommodate, as much as possible, people's individual work schedules.

In that way, companies would allow the employee to start sleeping in a manner that is much more compatible with their biology, rather than in conflict with it, which is what many of us seem to do in this modern world.

Of course, society is really designed for, and has a strong bias towards, the morning types. Perhaps unfairly so, since there truly is a wide range of natural preferences. Not everyone can wake up at 6am or earlier and function at their peak with grace, affability and aptitude.

Knowing this, by adapting society to our chronotypes rather than vice versa, we could have better-rested employees, better-rested leaders, and we know that more sleep equals more productivity. In addition, people utilise fewer healthcare resources when they're better slept. There could be manifold consequences.

There's a second theme worthy of note here, and it concerns immunity. What we know is that there's a very intimate relationship between your sleep health and your immune health. And one example, I think, has implications for the coronavirus going forward.

One study manipulated people's sleep in the week before they got a standard flu shot, shortening their sleep duration. The under-slept individuals went on to produce less than 50 per cent of the normal antibody response, relative to participants getting a full eight-hour sleep opportunity, rendering that vaccination far less effective for those sleep-deprived folks.

What's the idea for the future then? Well, perhaps we can start to enquire about people's sleep as they're coming in for their Covid vaccination. Could we enhance immunity – enhance the effectiveness of that vaccination – simply by coinciding it with a time when people are well slept?

Although we are only now beginning to investigate whether the same sleep-sensitivity is seen for the collection of Covid vaccines we now have, it seems like a more-than-prescient idea for the future. Especially considering how weakened our immune system becomes when we are not getting the sleep we need.

Put simply, sleep is the elixir of life – the Swiss Army knife of health, as it were. And from a business perspective, sleep is the greatest form of physiologically-injected venture capital that any company could wish for. With that, I bid you goodnight, and good sleep.

HENRY DIMBLEBY

RETHINKING
HOW WE EAT

Several of our contributors discuss food or the natural world. Restaurateur and food writer Henry Dimbleby connects the two. As he explains, the state exists to feed people. History suggests that when people are hungry, war follows – or even civilisational collapse. The historian Felipe Fernández-Armesto is among those to have shown many tribes or cultures disappeared because of hunger. The Natufians of Syria, the first sedentary civilisation, ran out of food 14,000 years ago. The invaders who conquered the Aztecs did so by cutting off their supplies. China's Ming dynasty came to power in large part because of a famine. The prospect of famine was a factor in the British leaving India after the bloody amputation of Partition.

Food, then, is a marker of civilisation: its health and its prospects. In our time, the next food crisis is both inevitable and unpredictable. Food crises are of two kinds; first, those brought on by shocks, such as pandemics; second, the rolling turmoil of what happens when we dump carbon in the sky, which food production does a lot of. Feeding a growing popula-

243

tion without scorching the earth will require new technologies, and Dimbleby mentions several. But the first requirement is a much greater sensitivity to the moral consequences of the journey made from farm to fork.

Britain's food system has just endured its biggest stress test since the Second World War. One symptom was obvious to everyone: the supermarket shelves stripped bare by people stockpiling as the Covid-19 pandemic swept west towards us. As I write, supermarket shelves are now almost fully stocked again but this doesn't mean there was never anything to worry about and it certainly doesn't mean we can afford to be complacent. Another crisis will hit the food system, possibly quite soon. When it does, it will probably look nothing like this one. Next time, it is most likely to be climate related. And whereas this crisis mainly affected the demand side of the economy, with the lockdown forcing an abrupt shift in the way we bought much of our food, climate change is more likely to affect supply.

One worst-case scenario would be the failure of multiple harvests in, say, China, India and Indonesia. If this happened, there might not be enough food to go around and when there is not enough food to go around, war usually follows. Our current food system is not well prepared for the dangers of climate change. Worse, it is a major contributor to the problem. Globally, the production and distribution of food is responsible for 25 to 30 per cent of greenhouse gases. From the energy used to manufacture fertiliser, to the methane emitted by rice paddies and ruminants, to the trucks driving our food to its final destination – every part of the system releases carbon.

As the pandemic hit, I was working on a national food strategy for the government, which aims to rethink how the whole food system should work, from farm to fork. I soon found that the debate about the future of food, like so many debates these days, has become fiercely polarised. The writer Charles C. Mann has described it as a stand-off between two hostile tribes, the wizards and the prophets. The wizards, coarsely put, believe that scientific innovation will rescue us from climate disaster so that we can carry on producing and consuming at much the same rate. And the prophets believe that we are living so far beyond the planet's means that we must drastically reduce consumption in order to survive.

But it seems to me that our real hope lies in diversity, both practical and ideological. A diverse system in which there are lots of different ways to produce food is more flexible. If one part of the system gets struck by disaster, the others can pick up the slack. By letting many flowers bloom, we can develop methods of farming and food production that better suit our rapidly changing world. In my future food-topia, I want to see organic farms as well as solar-powered high-rise greenhouses growing fruit and vegetables in cities. Rewilded landscapes as well as traditional upland farms. I want to see us consciously invest in the quality of our soil and in our biodiversity and I want massive investment in agricultural science and innovation, so that all farms can increase their yields without slathering the earth in chemicals.

In my food-topia, weed-picking robots and blight-spotting drones will become as much a part of the landscape as cattle from local native breeds, restored to their natural environment. We will still get our sustenance from the seas and the land, but also at vastly reduced carbon cost, from proteins fermented in vats fed by solar power. Instead of using pesticides, we will use epigenetics to switch on the immune systems of crops as a natural defence against harmful diseases. None of this is science fiction; these are all real innovations currently being developed in universities across this country. We must rebuild the food system so that it can survive climate change and stop contributing to it. For that, we will need the wisdom of both wizards and prophets. Only by bringing true diversity into food and farming can we build a system for the future.

Eliza Manningham-Buller

RETHINKING HEALTH INEQUALITY

Baroness Manningham-Buller rose to public prominence as the Director of MI5, the British internal security service. But it is her later work as chair of the remarkable Wellcome Trust, one of the biggest medical trusts in the world, that drives the searing and urgent message of this essay.

Manningham-Buller details the shocking disparities in life expectancy and susceptibility to disease that this ghastly virus has highlighted. Her essay is a blast of invective against inequality as it plays out in our health. And to think: it comes from a life peer in a country whose National Health Service, for all its faults, has risen to this occasion. If health inequality in Britain is a scandal, then further afield it's something much, much worse.

Health outcomes are a very powerful expression of underlying social and economic conditions. Every minute of every day, our health service is asked to deal with the consequences of inequality. I am struck by our essayist's perhaps unsurpris-

ing – and certainly unsentimental – emphasis on practical action and enlightened self-interest. And isn't her profound final thought, that any vaccine must not be hogged by the rich, the ultimate test by which the health of our nation will be judged?

There is a long way to go in the pandemic but we can now recognise the opportunity to build something better from the wreckage. The world has shifted and that provides the impetus for us to change and to protect our planet, its inhabitants and its once rich but now declining biodiversity.

I focus on the health of us, those human inhabitants. The differences in health, in the UK and throughout the world are clear, long-standing and indefensible. Health inequality has been graphically shown by the disproportionate way that the virus has attacked people. Those from the most deprived parts of the UK have died at nearly double the rate of those from the richest. People from ethnic minority backgrounds have suffered particularly badly. And in areas of the world where life is precarious and healthcare inadequate these inequalities are even more marked. But we should not be surprised as we have known for decades that deprivation in housing, employment and education all reduce life expectancy and contribute to disease. Boys born in Chelsea can expect to live to their mid-eighties: it can be ten years less in poorer areas. And in Nigeria, for example, you are very lucky to reach your sixties.

The pandemic reaches us all as it spreads round the world but we are far from equally affected. Where health-care systems are weak or non-existent, many will die. Because of the virus, millions of children are likely to miss their vaccinations and other diseases will be untreated. Loss of livelihoods will lead to cases of starvation.

I saw a poster held aloft at a recent anti-racist demon-stration. It read 'Injustice Anywhere – A Threat to Justice Everywhere'. I should like to borrow the sentiment behind that. 'Disease Anywhere – A Threat to Health Everywhere.' Infectious disease does not recognise national boundar-ies so nationalism can't address it.

What gives me hope is that it is clear that a broader range of governments, some pharmaceutical companies, and an increasing number of businesses, as well as many, many people now understand the need to work together for the collective good. It was encouraging, for example, that so many world leaders contributed to the Covid pledging conference held in May 2020 which raised nearly 10 billion euros for further investment in vaccines, treatments and diagnostics. It is encouraging that so many countries have allocated their excess vaccines to the COVAX initiative.

Common humanity should press us to work to reduce health inequalities wherever we find them but it's also in our self-interest to do so to disrupt the transmission of disease. If we are able – and it's absolutely possible, not least with digital medicine – to improve health everywhere, we will all benefit. And we must start by insisting that any treatments and vaccines which may be found for Covid are shared fairly and not hogged by the rich.

XINE YAO

RETHINKING
MASKS

Students of Elizabethan drama are familiar with the meta-
phorical power of masks on stage. They are the disguises that
can reveal something crucial about the disguised; the deceitful
top layer that contains a deeper truth.

Dr Xine Yao's essay is nothing less than a riveting journey
through cultural differences and interpretations. I'd better not
give it away but for now, suffice to say, that when an East
Asian person wears a mask in East Asia, they signal something
very different to when they wear it in, say, modern Britain.
And the same goes for those black people who, for reasons you
may not have considered until now, wear masks at marches.

To be frank with you, I just hadn't given enough thought to
the fact that in East Asia, masks are an expression of commit-
ment to the collective good; whereas if the same person wore
a mask (pre-pandemic) in, say, central London, it might be
alienating. It begs so many more questions. How are cultural
norms created? Why do stereotypes grip our imagination so?
And if, as seems necessary, we all have to get more used to

wearing them, and so become slightly more East Asian, might we put aside our prejudices when East Asians wear them in our midst?

W hat do you think now when you see someone wearing a mask?

The coronavirus crisis has transformed the medical mask from a device worn by many East Asians that was seen as a curiosity by the rest of the world into a global phenomenon. However, since masks conceal our faces from one another, they frustrate our efforts to express ourselves and connect with others. They act as uncomfortable visual reminders of social distancing and self-isolation. Nevertheless, we should recognise the necessity of wearing them for the sake of our own health and for the sake of the health of others. Masks are prompting us not only to reassess our everyday hygiene, but also to rethink about how we judge people's facial expressions – especially when they cannot be seen.

In the media, images of mask-wearing East Asians are synonymous with the coronavirus and reinforce Trump's 'Chinese virus' nickname for Covid-19. Ironically, we owe the development of medical masks to a Chinese-Malaysian doctor, Wu Lien-teh. He invented and promoted the practice of mask-wearing during the Manchuria Plague of 1910. Mask-wearing later became pervasive across Asia due to state regulations and subsequent outbreaks like

SARS. Although in Asia masks are understood as a collective good, elsewhere this protective measure is perceived as alienating: masks exacerbate stereotypes of East Asians as indistinguishable, unfeeling and deceptive. Paradoxically then, East Asians are more likely to be attacked as scapegoats for spreading the virus when they are wearing masks for everyone's protection. We tend to evaluate facial expressions as the representation of a person's true self, thus it is unsettling when masks reduce our ability to read faces. Yet is this always such a bad thing?

To wear or not to wear: who feels they are immune and who is disproportionately vulnerable? Lockdown protestors do not wear masks: notably, they are predominantly white and able-bodied. To them, masks are symbolic and physical barriers to their individual freedom of expression.

By contrast, many black people are worried they will be suspected of being criminals if they wear masks – and, as Black Lives Matter underlines, these stereotypes can be fatal. On the one hand, not wearing a mask might prevent racist backlash; on the other hand, that may expose them to the coronavirus when black people are already at greater risk of death because of structural inequalities. This mask dilemma reflects a general expectation that goes back to the struggle for abolition. When black people express their emotions and speak out, that functions as a powerful political tool for justice, but often the assumed conditions for them to be considered sympathetic preys upon their emotional vulnerability. Barriers like the mask block that expected access, stigmatising them as unsympathetic and dangerous.

As the world recovers, perhaps mask-wearing will become a more common practice of public hygiene. I wonder if this is an opportunity to re-examine our social and ethical norms about who and what we consider antisocial. The crisis has highlighted the importance of intimacy and transparency – but can we simultaneously accept the significance of withholding and concealment?

GEORGE SOROS

RETHINKING DEBT

The opening decades of the twenty-first century have not been very kind to economists who cling to convention. Few foresaw the financial crash of 2007–8. Since then, many of the tools that chancellors have traditionally sharpened to improve the economy seem to have been blunted. Monetary policy is simply not as useful as it used to be. Record jobs figures conceal deep anxieties about the quality and security of work. GDP reveals little about the roots of discontent.

Soros, a billionaire investor and philanthropist, was born shortly after the Wall Street Crash. He has witnessed countless economic cycles and crashes – but nothing that comes close to the economic devastation wreaked by the pandemic. A radical rethink is the only solution, and Soros has two specific proposals.

There is so much to admire in his analysis. First, sensitivity to different languages: the German word for debt, Schuld, which also means sin or guilt, is part of the psychological drama of modern Europe. Second, the coalition-building mindset that says, 'If we get the Dutch on board by talking them round, the Germans will follow.' And finally, the deep compassion that drives his argument. Soros was 90 in August

2020. He has given most of his life to giving money away. Few men of his generation speak with greater authority.

We live at a transformational moment in history. The range of possibilities is far greater than in normal times. At times like this, it is easier to influence events than to understand what is going on.

As a consequence, outcomes are unlikely to correspond to people's expectations. In other words, imperfect understanding, or fallibility, reigns supreme, and people become confused, disoriented and fearful of what lies ahead. Fear is a very bad advisor; it makes you do things that are bad for yourself and bad for the world.

At the very beginning of 2020, when Iranian General Soleimani was assassinated in Iraq, I realised that we had entered a global crisis that would change the direction of history. Then came Covid-19, which thoroughly disrupted people's lives all over the world.

What direction will history take? That is a question nobody can answer because the future depends on decisions that have not yet been taken. Nevertheless, I believe my Open Society Foundations and I are well situated to come up with ideas that can make the world a better place. Let me mention two of them that are of global importance.

The first idea is that the International Monetary Fund should issue a new round of Special Drawing Rights (SDR) and rich countries should donate their allocations which they don't need to poor countries that are in desperate need of them.

The second idea is, the European Union should issue perpetual bonds or Consols – the only financial instrument that could provide the EU with sufficient funds to successfully tackle the twin threats of Covid-19 and climate change.

Neither of them are my ideas; I merely recognised their importance and made them our priority. Both of them are very much alive and gaining increasing attention and support. The big question is whether they will be introduced soon enough because they are desperately needed – the SDR in the developing world and Consols in Europe. SDR are already in use and, at the time of writing only the veto of the Trump administration stands in the way of a new issue.

Consols face a bigger hurdle. They have been used by the UK and the US for centuries but they are a new idea for the EU and they challenge the deeply held belief prevalent in Germany that debts should always be repaid. The German word *Schuld* means both debt and guilt. I believe the Dutch, whose opposition to Consols is practical rather than ideological, could be convinced of the merits of Consols. The cost/benefit ratio of Consols is ten times better than the long-term bonds that the EU is planning to issue. If the Dutch change their minds the German will become easier to persuade.

Mariana Mazzucato

RETHINKING VALUE

It was in the comedy Lady Windermere's Fan, *which had the subtitle* A Play About a Good Woman, *that Oscar Wilde gave his celebrated definition of cynicism. A character called Lord Darlington quipped that a cynic was 'a man who knows the price of everything and the value of nothing'. Well, if you read enough of the economist Mariana Mazzucato's influential thinking, you might conclude we are all cynics now.*

In this philosophically agile challenge to economic models that have dominated post-war policy, Mazzucato provides three distinct types of value that need to be revived. She is the sort of economist who, even if you disagree with her – and many will – you can't ignore her.

Her essay put me in mind of a seminal work by the late Gertrude Himmelfarb, whose book The De-Moralisation of Society – *which put a hyphen in the word 'de-moralisation' – was subtitled* From Victorian Virtues to Modern Values. *She was writing more about ethics than economics, but despite her very different politics to Mazzucato, she shared with her a scepticism towards how we understand value. Mazzucato's essay can be read partly as a response to Oscar Wilde's Lord Darlington. I prefer to read it as a response to Himmelfarb; as nothing less, indeed, than the re-moralisation of economics.*

The health pandemic that we are going through has revealed an extreme weakness in the type of economy that we've built, but there's nothing inevitable about this type of economy. We can absolutely reshape it.

Over the last few months, our health systems have been revealed as too weak and under-resourced. During a crisis, there's no point in just throwing money at the NHS in the UK, or whatever health system we're in, if over the last decade it has been under-resourced, understaffed and demoralised. An extreme weakness in our work structures has also been exposed. A gig economy has left so many in jobs that have absolutely no protection, leaving them in very precarious situations. In addition, it's been revealed that in many cases – not all – governments have lacked the capacity and the capability to actually govern the crisis, whether this be in regard to the digital dimension, the health dimension or the communication with citizens themselves.

We should also remember that this particular crisis, which is a health crisis, actually occurs on the back of two others.

First of all, there is the climate one. So back in January, in February, we were not clapping health workers but fire workers in California and Australia, flood workers in Venice – and that climate crisis is just as strong if not even worse today. Also, there is an economic crisis. We experienced a massive financial crash back in 2008, the worst since 1929. And we still haven't recovered from that, both in terms of the rates of growth in many countries and also the direction of growth. Unfortunately, we did not learn the mistakes of an ultra-financialised economy, where the financial sector itself has mainly been fuelling other parts of the financial sector – finance, insurance and real estate – rather than funnelling funds into real production structures that can also help us solve some of the most pressing challenges of today.

So I want to propose that this moment is a massive wake-up call for us that requires us to deal with the underlying structures of these problems, otherwise we will continue to lurch from one crisis to the next. And I believe it's quite useful to think about these underlying structures in terms of a new conversation, new framing and new tools to confront what we mean by 'value'. So the concept of value can be almost an organising device for us to think about the future. I'm going to break that down into three dimensions.

The first is we need to recognise that we have not learned yet how to value our common resources. You can think of this as the global public goods. Back to the issue of healthcare: unfortunately, in our economy we only know how to value those areas to which we can give a monetary value. This means that areas like public education or public health often aren't valued. You can see this by how little teachers are paid in state schools and also in attitudes to health workers themselves. And because the benefits of a properly funded health system come to us all, we actually don't know how to put the value of that into GDP. We only put in the costs – the costs of hospitals, the costs of health care, the costs of a teacher – but we don't know how to *value* the benefits. In fact, it doesn't count in how we measure growth in our economy.

The second value in terms of what we can achieve together is a collective value creation process. It's extraordinary how in moments of emergency we do come together, but it doesn't actually last in terms of learning, or in terms of really bringing together the full force of the public sector, the private sector, the third sector and citizen groups, to solve some of the greatest problems of our time. And Covid, in fact, has thrown to us many different problems, not only those related to health, but also, for example, those related to the digital divide, which affects those students who are at home today, not going to school. They're not all being educated equally; so much depends on the resources they have in their lives. In addition, there's the loneliness of the elderly at home and, coming back to the issues of health, the race for a vaccine is not going to happen just by one actor alone, whether it's the state or the private sector. A massive collaboration is required.

And that brings me to my third point about value, which is what do we actually mean by stakeholder value? There's been a lot of talk about this. I was in Davos in January and it was all about bringing purpose back to the company, purpose back to our capitalist system, and the term 'stakeholder value' was used to identify that. But this is the moment with this health pandemic to really test whether all that talk about purpose and stakeholder value is matched with the walk. It's not enough to have a race for a vaccine. We absolutely need both public and private sectors to work together in that collaborative way I was just talking about, and we also need to govern that process in such a way that it really does produce a public good.

A stakeholder value approach needs to break down the details of how we work together in the public interest. So, for example, with a vaccine it's absolutely essential that we pool our intellectual property. That we have more of a solidarity and less of a competitive framework in terms of how we produce health innovation. It also means that we could require strong conditions to be placed around the bailouts. Many different companies across different sectors are receiving a lot of money from the government because of the stress that they are under – for example, aeroplanes not flying, hotels not having any bookings, etc. But those bailouts should occur in a stakeholder value approach with a real sense of give and take between both parties. So, for example, conditions for the airlines could actually be matched by the sector reducing its carbon emissions. This is something that has been done in France with Air France and, in Denmark, they've been talking about having the bailouts conditional on companies not using tax havens.

So this third point is really how do we learn from Covid and, in this moment where governments are being asked to put so much money on the table, how do we really work together in the stakeholder governance approach that actually allows a long-term vision for an economy? What we need is for an economy to be more inclusive, more sustainable, to actually help us design the new contracts and the new social contract between business and government.

So, just to come back to the first point. I am just really hoping that this moment which is presenting such stress to so many different people – in fact, everyone, I think is undergoing a very difficult time – I hope it will actually help us redesign the type of capitalism we want. There is nothing inevitable, there's nothing determined in our current structures; we can redesign them. And this is a massive wake-up call that we must do that.

Douglas Alexander

RETHINKING ECONOMIC DIGNITY

It is often argued today that western politics has moved beyond the class distinctions that defined it in the twentieth century. According to this thesis, voters today sort into socio-cultural rather than socio-economic tribes. Attitudes towards change, or belonging, or national pride are better predictors of voting patterns than whether you're rich or poor. Indeed, in British politics, a remarkable realignment has happened: the Conservative Party is no longer the party of the rich, and Labour is no longer the party of the poor. The two 'masses' of post-war British politics – mass demographic upheaval and mass higher education – have caused this historic upending.

Moreover, the Labour Party was founded as the parliamentary representation of the working class; but the working class no longer exists, certainly in the sense that Marx and Engels meant the phrase in the mid-nineteenth century. For one thing, manual labour – selling physical exertion for a wage – is a much smaller part of our economy; for another, the institutions that protected and promoted the old working class, from trade unions to friendly societies, are in abeyance. The working class has given way to an atomised, alienated poor.

Much of this argument holds, but the response to it from many of the smartest thinkers on the left and centre-left is the same. Namely: this is true, but the work of economic justice is not yet done. Here, Douglas Alexander provides a cogent corrective to the cultural turn in our politics and, to his credit, it includes practical policy suggestions.

Sometimes you just don't notice something until it's gone.

When the Covid-19 pandemic swept across the UK it brought many hardships, not least of which was families being separated from their loved ones. For many months I could not sit with my mum and dad nor reach out and hug them. When I could no longer visit their care home, people who our society often take for granted stepped in and provided the expertise, companionship and protection that my parents needed to keep them safe.

Throughout the crisis, care workers, cleaners, shelf stackers and refuse collectors got up every day and did their jobs – often at great risk to their own health. Jobs which we applauded on our doorsteps but which are routinely underestimated, undervalued and underpaid. What the pandemic exposed is that our society relies on these workers the most, and yet our economy pays them the least. In truth, the UK's 4.2 million low-paid workers have an underlying condition. It's called poverty.

So we now need a rethink that leads to a new settlement. What do we want to value as a society?

My parents' care has been literally priceless, yet every day, low-paid workers are made to feel worthless. They're told their work is low skilled, meriting only a low wage. That's not just wrong. It's immoral.

The new settlement that we need is about culture and esteem as well as politics and economics. If we value, and reward only one category of jobs – the 'head' jobs – we'll never improve the status and rewards of essential jobs that need heads, hearts and hands.

We need the moral courage to turn doorstep applause into practical actions. Actions like extending statutory sick pay to all lower earners, and establishing a pay review body to raise care sector pay. Actions like empowering and protecting all workers with access to trade union support and the right to choose whether to be paid weekly, fortnightly or monthly.

Economic dignity isn't too much to ask for essential work.

Just over 50 years ago, Martin Luther King spoke in support of sanitation workers striking over decent wages. Prophetically, King told the crowd: 'One day our society will come to respect the sanitation worker if it is to survive, for the person who picks up our garbage, in the final analysis, is as significant as the physician. For if he doesn't do his job, diseases are rampant. All labour has dignity.'

Fifty years on, that remains the essential truth about essential workers. The battle against the virus would be betrayed if we do not also win the battle against low pay. We must reshape the common good with common sense. The new normal must be based on a new settlement, that delivers economic dignity for low-paid workers.

Evan Spiegel

RETHINKING LONG-TERM SUCCESS

Perhaps the greatest weakness of democracy is short-termism. Political cycles, being so brief, incentivise policies that lead to re-election, rather than long-term betterment.

Rivals to democracy have countless flaws, but are often freer to look at the horizon. In their speeches today, the rulers of China, Russia and India – arguably an autocracy, a kleptocracy, and the world's biggest and most fragile democracy respectively – make very clear that they think in vast stretches of time. They see that you can have a bad few centuries, and then a good few. And they think they are due the latter.

In other words, they are epochalists. And in this frame of mind they are joined by many of the most enterprising minds within western democracy too. Jeff Bezos and Elon Musk constantly talk about human civilisation. The former is building the Clock of the Long Now, a clock that keeps time for 10,000 years inside a mountain. The latter is a fan of the computer game Civilization, *and, like Bezos, is working on colonisation of space. Mark Zuckerberg lauds Augustus, the Roman Emperor, because he secured 200 years of peace.*

Such perspective helps us understand ourselves, and each other. Evan Spiegel's essay shows he is an epochal thinker too, and in the best sense of that term. I share his core analysis here: the view that the West has now entered a new, third chapter, following the Keynesian triumph of the New Deal and post-war Britain, and then the triumph of free-market economics around the start of the 1980s.

Moreover, the image of America as 'a start-up, nearly 250 years young,' is irresistible. Younger than most tech billionaires, Spiegel embodies the entrepreneurial zeal of California today, and his argument implies a profound challenge to democrats and elected officials everywhere, to think beyond not just the next ballot, but their lifetimes too.

My favourite question is a simple one. Over the years, I've asked it whenever I have the chance, inviting millennials and baby boomers, academics and public servants, business leaders, friends and colleagues to engage with the same 13-word prompt:

What is your vision for success in America over the next 100 years?

For some, national success hinges on outcomes – the eradication of poverty or acceleration of upward mobility. Others cite a true reckoning with their national story, or a range of structural reforms to the criminal-legal, healthcare and education systems. Philosophically inclined respondents often tie success to an ongoing pursuit of founding values.

At 30 and still at the beginning of my own learning journey, I am asking this question not to arrive at a single answer, but because I've observed that we have become overly focused on short-term metrics, such as GDP, that improperly measure our national progress. We define success in a way that devalues the investments most likely to unlock our latent human potential in the coming century.

As economists Nathaniel Hendren and Ben Sprung-Keyser have shown, critical long-term investments – like early childhood education or health – yield hugely positive returns, generally paying for themselves over the course of decades. But because we make decisions by looking at five- or 10-year budget windows, we distort the decision-making architecture that would otherwise enable longer-run thinking. The result? In America, the federal government spends approximately $1 on each kid for every $6 on a senior (according to calculations by the Committee for a Responsible Federal Budget and the Urban Institute).

Yet some of the most transformative and memorable achievements in American history – like the moon landing or the internet – have been the result of public investments that pay dividends over many years. And they are often achieved by people working together to prioritise collective success over individual interests.

An emphasis on the long-term is not intended to take anything away from the urgency of today's most pressing issues. Education, healthcare and housing are unacceptably out of reach for millions. And governments are uniquely positioned to make the foundational investments that could address these challenges. But without being guided by a shared vision for future success, it is difficult to invite collaboration across generations of leaders to solve these major problems.

America has arguably been shaped by two 'big ideas' over the past century. President Franklin Roosevelt's New Deal inspired an era of government spending and social welfare policies. Decades later, President Ronald Reagan embraced an economic approach that centred on government itself as the 'problem'.

We may now be on the eve of our next consequential rethink. Many young people in the United States – myself included – have lived through the 9/11 terrorist attacks, the 2008 global financial crisis and, now, a global pandemic. We are approaching the limits of America's small-government, cut-taxes-to-promote-growth, individualised-self-interest approach to future success.

I like to think of America as a start-up, nearly 250 years young, in a world full of nations that have been around far longer. Whatever success may look like to each of us, we are part of something bigger. And that means we must share a long-term vision and invest strategically to secure our future.

WHERE
WE GO

PETER FRANKOPAN

RETHINKING ASIA

In the introduction, I noted that Easternisation was one of the giant forces shaping the epoch into which we are stumbling. This is the Age of Asia – and outside Asia, few authors have explained what that means as cogently as Peter Frankopan.

His seminal book, The Silk Roads, *which sold over a million copies, made the case for an understanding of our common past that is much more rooted in the vast stretches of land that connect the Pacific Ocean to the Middle East. The domination of Europe and its cultural progeny – that is, the West – is, he noted, a recent aberration in the grand sweep of global history.*

The great virtue of his essay is that it makes the case for Asia as the focus of the global future, too. The eastward shift in power, and therefore conflict, could define this century. And the sheer scale of challenges in places like China and India is hard for the western imagination to fathom.

Have we even tried? I was born in Calcutta, have a huge family in India, and take a close interest in Asian affairs. Yet Frankopan's essay sets a series of quiz questions which, I am mortified to admit, I completely flunked. How will you get on?

I travel a lot to Asia – or at least I used to, before lock-downs meant that long-distance travel turned into a decent walk in the local park. Those walks, though, have given me a chance to reflect on 30 years of astonishing change, of modernisation, urbanisation and ambition since the fall of the Berlin Wall, the opening up of China and a period of intense and intensive globalisation.

I've been lucky to witness much of this first-hand. But I also know that for many, it will be hard to 'Rethink Asia' when we spend so little time thinking about Asia in the first place. Despite being the world's largest and most populated continent, knowledge about the peoples, regions and cultures lying to the east of Istanbul and stretching as far as the Indian and Pacific Oceans is limited and basic – at best.

If you ask anyone who the most significant British, French or American person in history is, you'll get a long list of suggestions. Ask for the name of a single Chinese Emperor, of any influential author in pre-colonial South Asian literature, or any of the architects who designed the glorious monuments of some of the great cities and imperial capitals on the planet – like Damascus, Isfahan, Samarkand or Huế – and you'll be met with silence.

As a historian, it amazes me how little interest we have in the past beyond the familiar stories of kings and queens close to home. After all, Asia was home to the world's first empires; it is where all our major global religions come from; it was economically and culturally dominant until the rise of Europe around 300 years ago – a mere heartbeat in historical terms. And yet the western intellectual tradition has essentially written Asian history, politics and culture out of the story of the past.

That makes it difficult, if not impossible, to understand the present. The opportunities – and challenges – of the twenty-first century do not lie in Europe or the West. The battle to save the world's climate will not be fought by improving recycling in Oslo or Phoenix, Arizona, but in Asia, home to all 50 of the planet's most polluted cities – and all but a tiny handful of the top 500. The struggle to improve global poverty, health, education and equality, likewise, will be at its sharpest in mega-cities with high population densities, infrastructure pressures and high energy, water and resource requirements. These too are disproportionately located in Asia. It is in Asia that globalisation has delivered its greatest blessings and come at the highest environmental cost.

The tectonic plates of the world are shifting today partly because of new technologies. But we are also entering an age where the role and nature of the state are becoming once again a question of profound importance if not of anxiety. In many (but not all) countries in Asia, the direction of travel looks very different to that of the developed western world. We need to spend more time understanding where this is happening and why, and to work out what the implications are for ourselves.

As all good professors like to say, it helps if one does one's homework. When it comes to Asia, we could and must all do better.

RETHINKING AI

For several years now, there has been a growing panic about artificial intelligence. And not without good reason: the computational power that we have already developed is not only astonishing, but it does force us to ask ourselves what makes us, as Homo sapiens, unique; and, moreover, what we want our relationship with technology to be. In short: how can humanity make use of technology, rather than – as countless science fiction authors have wondered – the other way round?

One great consolation for people worried about the march of AI lies in the distinction between consciousness and intelligence. The former is our capacity to feel things like pleasure, pain, hope and despair. The latter is a capacity for problem solving. AI can do the latter but not the former. This is reassuring, and also makes clear the social, medical and other dilemmas that AI can help us with. Such is the acceleration in the development of AI today, that legal and moral quandaries we have never given sufficient thought to are now urgent and unavoidable. In this powerful argument, Professor Russell laments how slowly we have learned to make the most of AI, *and finishes by suggesting two radical ideas to ensure that AI is a net benefit, rather than cost, to humanity.*

I work on artificial intelligence. I also have some familiarity with medicine, as a faculty member in neurosurgery. And by working on the nuclear test ban treaty, I have learned something about global monitoring and global cooperation. My current focus is on safe, beneficial co-existence between humans and increasingly powerful AI systems, which will also turn out to be relevant.

I'm often asked, 'Can AI solve the Covid crisis?' No. It's mostly biology and medicine and public health. AI can help with early detection of epidemics, fusing information from many sources to see patterns that no one doctor can easily perceive. AI can also help with decision-making: when and where to impose quarantines, whom to test, when and what to reopen and how to adjust the process on the fly. To help in the current crisis, however, we and AI should have started ten years ago. Even if the technical problem can be solved in a few months, it takes years more to establish confidence, gain agreement from governments and put the systems in place.

So, the next question is why didn't we do it ten years ago? First, the broad AI community is very focused on cool toys and making money. The concern about 'AI for good' is quite recent. Second, there's always a sense that really bad things can't happen because the grown-ups will take care of it. We have to grow up ourselves and learn this lesson: that the cost of prevention is far lower than the cost of failure to prevent. For this epidemic it may be 10,000 times lower. It's common sense; it's why we have smoke detectors and fire extinguishers. The epidemiologists have been warning us for years that the big one was coming, and we have ignored them.

Post-Covid, I hope we can have rational discussions about the major risks we face and how to prevent them. Not just pandemics but also climate change, nuclear war, and even asteroid collisions. In my own field, there's a vigorous debate about how we can retain control – *forever* – over AI systems that will eventually become more powerful than us. I hope that the AI community and the governments that fund it will stop saying, 'But really bad things can't happen because the grown-ups will take care of it.' The solution I've proposed is a different way of designing AI systems that makes them necessarily beneficial to humans. And that means beneficial not to one particular human or corporation or government, but to all of us, the human race. Clearly, we are in this together.

If I could ask for one change for the better, it would be a return to a belief in the value of international cooperation. There is a form of insanity infecting the world right now that views any international agreement as a restriction of national sovereignty. That's like demanding the right to drive on both sides of the road. We'd all have more vehicular sovereignty, but the roads would be a disaster and everyone would be worse off. That's exactly the situation we are in now. I hope we can do better. In the immediate aftermath, for example, we must agree on and implement global monitoring and response mechanisms for infectious diseases. And I'd like to put two personal requests onto the agenda for global agreement. First, enshrining a human right to know if we are communicating with another human or a machine. And second, banning machines that can decide to kill humans.

V.S. RAMACHANDRAN

RETHINKING BRAINS

Within the past few centuries alone there have been several small scientific revolutions. Few are more exciting than the neuroscientific revolution of the past two decades. Our understanding of the brain has grown exponentially. And nobody has done more to drive our knowledge forward, or to bring it to the masses, than former Reith Lecturer Vilayanur S. Ramachandran.

This son of Tamil Nadu (full disclosure: my dad is Tamilian too) synthesises for us here some of the key lessons he has gleaned through his recent work in neurology labs. One of the main insights is the degree to which we have evolved to tell a coherent story about ourselves, even in defiance of evidence presented to us. We are the self-narrativising ape, determined to apply a plot structure to events in which we are involved.

From this flows much of our daily interaction – and also clues as to how, in the world after Covid-19, we might use technology to do things very, very differently. Stick with Ramachandran here, because he ends on an optimistic note. Every day, neuroscience is delivering revelations that add wonder to our understanding of our brains, those magic machines each of us possess, which are the most complex objects in the known universe.

Right now, the world is facing a terrifying crisis. No one has ever seen anything like it before, except in horror movies in Hollywood. A deadly, highly contagious virus is transmitted from pangolin-like creatures to humans in Chinese markets. It then invades the lungs to produce a pneumonia that's often fatal. We soon start wondering, what's going to happen to us? To humanity? Where is the end? Right now, there are too many questions and unknowns about this virus to allow intelligent speculation and answers. Indeed, it's too early to make pronouncements of any kind, other than banal remarks about humankind's arrogance and utter disregard for Mother Nature. (Let's not forget, it was by 'tampering' with Mother Nature that we saved humankind from the scourge of smallpox using vaccination and of diphtheria and tuberculosis using antibiotics.) Leaving rhetoric aside, one thing is clear, things can never be the same again.

And things can happen at lightning speed. Before you even realise what's going on, in a matter of days, tiny wisps of jelly (RNA wrapped in protein) can all but decimate humankind. Astonishingly, most people throughout the world are indifferent to the magnitude of the problem, the sheer magnitude.

Why? Where does this denial come from anyway? In neurological patients, it's not unusual to encounter patients who are stubbornly assertive or even aggressive in their denial; we sometimes see these patients every other month in local hospitals. For example, a patient with a paralysed left hand following a right-hemisphere stroke will vehemently deny that his left arm is paralysed and sometimes deny that it belongs to him. He might even claim it belongs to his mother. This seems grotesque.

But guess what? We all engage in denial to some extent. There are hints from our research that conceptual/linguistic forms of denial are ordinarily mediated by the left hemisphere of the brain, which responds to sensory and cognitive discrepancies by using Freudian defence mechanisms. These mechanisms include things we all talk about like rationalisation, repression, outright denial, rejection. Our brains have evolved to create a consistent story, a narrative about ourselves with an artificially increased confidence and optimism, as you see in a car salesman. This serves to stabilise our behaviour and allows us to forge ahead and impress potential suitors, mates. Originally, it was useful – but denial is often overdone and if it's overdone, it can lead to maladaptive behaviour. In California, even a week into the shutdown, crowds were assembling and defiantly partying on the beach. So much for the eight-foot rule.

Fortunately, such delusional overconfidence of the left hemisphere is counterbalanced by a sceptical internal sensor. Your own devil's advocate in your right hemisphere. This is a gross oversimplification, of course, along with the mechanisms of denial and Freudian defences, but it's a place to start. Normally, these opposing forces of creative confabulation versus scepticism are in a state of constant, dynamic equilibrium. However, if the equilibrium is perturbed by a tumultuous upheaval in our physical and social wellbeing and in the environment in which we're immersed, the result can be devastating.

But let's pause for a second: not all is doom and gloom. The pandemic has already changed the way we think about the future and about ourselves. It will make us question the axiomatic foundations of our lives, make us re-examine all our bourgeois values and lifestyles. The distinction between office, home, work and play is already dissolving as more and more people are talking of Zoomifying, Zoom parties, Zoom offices, Zoom cuddles, Zoom huddle rooms. You peel off the layers of maladaptive traditions as you go along. The quality and resolution of VR and TV is going to improve enormously, at an accelerated pace, to a point where it will be indistinguishable from reality. This will allow us to become close to others, but without the taboos and barriers that have been hypocritically attached to this so-called reality of ours, which we have to deal with every day.

This whole scheme reminds me of the movie *The Matrix*, its end point being Roald Dahl's notorious brain-in-a-vat scenario, where the brain is isolated and floating in a jar of nutrition and watching the world pass by passively. I'm already waking up, wondering whether I'm in Zoom or in real land and if so, is it in Rome, Chennai, London, Lahore? At the flick of a switch, I can be anywhere. To some people, this might seem fake, mere simulation. But so what? You are already brains in vats; each vat is a cranial cavity. Welcome aboard on our voyage to the new world and let the Zoom be with you.

Seb Emina

RETHINKING TRAVEL

Is there some way to get the benefits and joy of travel without, well, travelling? Those of us who have found foreign travel to be one of the great pleasures of life have, in recent years, felt ever more guilt. The fumes released by aeroplanes, and the height at which they are emitted, have a huge ecological cost. Building planes that are environmentally friendly is hard. The Swedes even have a word for it: *flygskam*, or 'flying shame'. Electric planes are hard to build: you need huge batteries, which might be 20 years away. But as Seb Emina explains, there are remarkable new technologies that can create the sensation of seeing the wonders of the world without literally seeing them. Can he persuade you?

The idea that what we seek when we travel isn't just the odd nice pyramid or unfamiliar cuisine, but a sense of disconnection from the noise of our lives, contains real wisdom. And to think, as Emina says, if we want to disconnect, we could just leave the house without our phones: that's a seductive idea. It might not be quite the same as sitting *on a beach in Jamaica, or the unforgettable moment when you first set eyes on the Taj Mahal. But I should really try it some time.*

I went to the Taj Mahal today. It was beautiful. When I say 'went' I mean virtually, of course. The most severe phase of lockdown may finally be easing up as I write this in summer 2020, but the idea of actual long-haul travel still seems laughable. I've become curious instead about a form of activity that, like flying cars or domestic robots, has always felt like it would signify having arrived in 'the future'. Namely that I might travel without actually leaving home, via some kind of incredibly convincing technological simulation.

The impetus to do so is not just pandemic-related. Knowing what we do about the environmental impact of aviation, it's becoming difficult to justify getting on a plane just because we want to see this great monument or behold that breathtaking natural wonder.

My Taj Mahal visit was facilitated through a simple virtual reality headset. I held it to my eyes and surveyed the seventeenth-century Mughal mausoleum. Tourists streamed past the camera. Music played. When I turned my head, the image turned with it. The clip was 90 seconds long. It was travel in the way that looking at a hologram on a postcard is travel. Which is to say, it wasn't really travel at all.

To be honest, it was quite boring. Virtual reality has a long way to go before it can authentically replicate the elusive assortment of activities we are talking about when we use words like 'travel' or 'holiday'. The dream is what's known in the business as 'full immersion' virtual reality, in which a fake experience will be impossible to distinguish from a real one.

Picture this: I steer a boat to some simulated caves in Chile. I not only see the damp cave walls and hear the growl of the boat's engine but I smell motor oil and feel cold drips falling from stalactites as they hit me on the cheek. Afterwards I return to a simulated hotel and go to sleep after ordering a simulated club sandwich.

If that all seems quite far-fetched – well, that's because it is. At least for now. On the other hand, researchers recently announced a prototype of what they call 'smart skin', which could enable the sensation of touch to be played back or broadcast by technological means, and there are start-ups in California hard at work on so-called 'brain machine interfaces' which might some day allow a beach on, say, the Greek island of Naxos to be beamed directly into our minds.

Which of course raises quite a few philosophical questions. If I know, deep down, that this beach is fake, won't it ruin my ability to sunbathe wholeheartedly, no matter how real it appears? And how am I supposed to track down whichever locals' cafe allows me to feel I have discovered the 'true Naxos'? Most importantly, in a world where we can inject sensory data directly into our consciousnesses, won't the concept of travel mean something completely different anyway?

In fact, when I think about that last question I find myself suspecting that virtual reality already exists. It just looks unsettlingly different from what we expected: not pixellated replicas of Niagara Falls but the perpetual info-torrent of social media. Haven't we each been surprised, during lockdown, by quite how much of our social life remained exactly as it was before? As our attentions are increasingly monopolised by the tricks of well-paid psychologists in Silicon Valley, I have this suspicion that the spirit of travel, or part of it, will become available simply by walking out of the front door, with no devices to hand.

Happily, that also doesn't involve getting on a plane.

Aaron Bastani

RETHINKING AN AGEING POPULATION

Close your eyes for a moment, please. Now – bear with me – think of a python that's swallowed a pig. Over time, as the vanquished pig moves slowly down the python's body, it's digested and gets smaller. You can open your eyes now. That was a metaphor. The python is a population in a country or region of the world. The pig is the youth bulge.

If this metaphor has caused you discomfort, I'm sorry; but a) it was worse for the pig; and b) the metaphor isn't mine. It belongs to David Willetts, the Conservative intellectual. He came up with it in a programme for Radio 4 about how demography, as I also argued in the introduction, is the secret engine of global history. Though he and Aaron Bastani have very different politics, this may be an issue that commands bipartisan support.

We are, as Bastani powerfully puts it, on the verge of one of the most extraordinary flips in human history, when there will be more old people than young people. And an explosion of old people in the West, and young people elsewhere, will be a defining feature of the epoch we are entering. It's fashionable to say demography isn't destiny; but to a significant degree it both is and will continue to be.

Even before the arrival of Covid-19, it was increasingly self-evident that ours is an era of crisis. Indeed, to say as much no longer strikes me as even remotely controversial; rather it borders on the cliché.

There is a crisis of rising inequality, within and between nations; this is exacerbated by technological trends where gains in productivity redound almost entirely to the already affluent and where monopolies drive out smaller business.

There is a crisis of ecology with a rise in global temperatures of at least two degrees this century viewed by many as now inevitable. While that in itself would be disastrous, the worst part is it would likely catalyse a sequence of feedbacks leading to yet higher temperatures still. A world three degrees warmer than today could see the Amazon face desertification, while the glaciers that provide clean drinking water for a third of the planet's population would disappear.

Finally, there is a crisis of political authority and legitimacy, as citizens around the world increasingly feel that power doesn't really reside in their elected representatives, and that politics itself is incapable of improving their lives. Here impotence is the default effect, often leading to fear, hopelessness and sometimes bigotry.

And yet the scale of all these crises, at least in the medium term, don't come close to an issue which even now garners surprisingly few headlines: demographic ageing. For the last 15,000 years, through flood, famine and war, the population of our species has only grown. By the end of this century it will likely peak at around 10 billion people.

Alongside this will be another change, one without precedent not only in human history but in the entirety of the natural world: the old will begin to outnumber the young. By 2050, those over 65 are set to outnumber those under 14. Today the average human can expect to reach 71 years of age, an improvement of four decades on just a century ago.

In 1900, the leading causes of death were primarily infection: influenza, cholera, smallpox. Today they are almost entirely age-related: heart disease, stroke, cancer and dementia. For such conditions ageing is the single biggest risk factor, with an 80-year-old 40 times more likely to die from cancer as someone in middle age, and their risk of Alzheimer's 600 times greater. While survival rates for these conditions – like cancer and heart disease – are steadily improving, that means ever greater resources will be expended on a minority of the population – what is termed the 'oldest old'. Between 2016 and 2030, Britain's over-65 population is set to increase by a third, while its oldest old, those over 85, will double. Already dementia, with its immense costs, is the UK's leading cause of death.

Caring for such a large number of people who exhibit the leading risk factor for conditions that are both labour- and resource-intensive, will require a major expansion in health and social care – and all at the same moment that working-age populations are shrinking and society must address other momentous challenges like climate change and inequality.

Indeed, the extent to which ageing will test our economic models and welfare systems is discernible from a simple figure: the ratio of those in work to those of retirement age. Today, across the world, there are 6.3 people of working age for every person over 65. The UN claims that figure will fall to 3.4 to 1 by 2050, and 2.4 to 1 by 2100.

For some countries the 'future' of demographic ageing, even accompanied by population decline, is already here. Portugal could lose up to half its population by 2060, and in 2015 fewer babies were born in Italy than in any year since 1861. But it is worst of all in Eastern Europe, a region which, according to the United Nations, has lost 6 per cent of its population since the early 1990s – some 18 million people.

Yet such shifts aren't limited to Europe and appear universal in scope. South Korea's birth replacement rate is just 1.2, meaning that by 2040 it will have a dependency ratio of three to one. Japan, which had a population of 128 million in 2010 (today it is 126 million) is expected to fall below 100 million by 2050, and 85 million by the end of the century. Indeed, according to some economists, its shrinking working-age population is 'one of the biggest causes of the long-term recession' Japan has faced since the mid 1990s. China, expected to be the world's largest economy before the end of this decade, is confronting an almost equally difficult task as a result of its one child policy. Demographic ageing even extends to geopolitics and it is likely the greatest obstacle to this being a 'Chinese Century'.

If Japan is an avatar of our collective future, what does that mean? Clearly it suggests economic inertia – something of rising concern to policymakers around the world as they begin to take seriously the prospect of 'secular stagnation' and permanently low growth. This is allied to rising debt, with a 2016 report by Standard and Poor, a credit ratings agency, claiming that 25 per cent of all countries could see their sovereign debt status reduced to 'junk' as a result of ageing by 2050 – with rising health and social care costs at the very moment the working-age population, and with it the national tax base, dramatically shrinks.

That same report concluded that by 2050 countries such as Brazil, China, Japan, Russia and Saudi Arabia will all see their levels of public debt rise as high as 250 per cent of GDP – and that was before Covid and its attendant economic downturn. Such an extraordinarily high figure is normally associated with the aftermath of war – and yet it will soon become the global norm simply as a result of people living longer and having fewer children.

In Britain, just the costs of health and long-term social care, the state pension and other elderly benefits are expected to increase annual spending by 2.5 per cent of GDP every year for the next decade. We are only at the beginning of this epochal trend and, already, health-care and pensions are the two largest expenses in Britain's budget, accounting for around 40 per cent of government spending in 2019.

So ageing societies will mean permanently lower growth and considerably more resources to health and social care. Already Covid-19 has offered the outline of one response to that: the chilling idea that the lives of the elderly are somehow less valuable than the young. I've heard that explicitly stated several times, most memorably on US television in arguments against a lockdown in the spring of 2020.

Yet for the vast majority of us – who place the worth of human life above GDP growth or a thriving stock market – this poses major problems. A future of economic expansion is, in no small part, dependent on the presumption that the young will always outnumber the old – just as they have for the last 200,000 years of human history. And yet, in this century, that will no longer be true.

The solution? A socialised national care service funded by progressive taxation. Yes, this will be extraordinarily expensive, and a historic policy innovation on a par with the creation of the NHS after 1945, but there isn't really an alternative if we are serious about the problem.

If we do that then care workers, who remain unappreciated no matter how many rounds of applause they get, can be paid what they are worth – and all while care itself becomes one of the few sectors to create jobs in the broader context of automation.

After the challenge of Covid-19 has been surmounted, which it will, we need to rethink care work and grasp that demographic ageing is every bit as big a challenge as climate change. Indeed, for the rest of our lives, it will likely be worse.

Business as usual has no chance of success and pursuing economic growth above all else will increasingly resemble a fanatical creed. Dispensing with the present orthodoxy is necessary while adult care must go from the margin of our social lives, and political priorities, to the centre.

Rana Foroohar
RETHINKING DATA

How did they get away with it? How did just five companies (with admittedly astounding products) manage to acquire so much wealth, and put it in the hands of so few, for so long? Historians will doubtless look at the first two decades of the twenty-first century, in which we witnessed the biggest asymmetry of knowledge, wealth and power ever seen, as a period when democracies failed to exert sufficient scrutiny on these kings of data – or extract enough tax from them. As I write in the introduction, several of the biggest challenges of the post-pandemic world involve reconciling the big tech companies to the interests, as opposed to just the needs, of citizens everywhere.

One reason that democracies everywhere have been so slow to exert control over these data giants is that regulation is national, consensual, slow and quickly dates, whereas the FAANGS are global and innovate very fast. The other reason, frankly, is that the FAANGS spend tens of millions of pounds lobbying governments. Economic analyst Rana Foroohar has a specific proposal there, for a new tax. Together with the idea that we should own our own data, that's two concrete ideas for a better world after Covid-19. Which government will be brave or bold enough to legislate for them?

Wealth inequality and the imbalance of power between capital and labour is the economic problem of our time. And this is a problem that has really been put on steroids by Covid-19. Even before the pandemic hit, since the late 1990s, corporate concentration has increased to such a level that 80 per cent of corporate wealth is now being held in just 10 per cent of firms. And those are the firms that are rich in digital data and intellectual property. They tend to be concentrated in three industries, tech, finance and pharma, which have seen their profits triple since the late 1990s. But amongst those, the biggest and most powerful companies are the FAANGs: Facebook, Amazon, Apple, Netflix, Google. These companies control more wealth and power than the entire economy of France and of course, since the pandemic, these are the companies that we have come to depend on. They are essential. They are delivering our goods, they're helping us to do our video conferences and helping us to shop online.

But the problem is every time we go online, every time we're on the internet, on our mobile phones, on that video conference, our personal data is being harvested by these companies. Data is the oil of the new economy and the companies get it for free. They also benefit from the network effect. They can go in and quickly grab market share, undercutting competitors and then using their disproportionate profits to buy up other companies that might threaten them in the marketplace. These companies, of course, also have disproportionate lobbying power. They are amongst the largest corporate lobbyists in places like Washington and Brussels and that has allowed them to locate profits wherever they like, to shift regulations to suit them.

We know that self-regulation in technology, as in finance, doesn't work. Anti-trust action has finally come in places like the US and Europe, and we may eventually see a break-up of some of the FAANGs and the big tech giants. But such cases take years. We need a rebalancing of that digital divide, of that divide between labour and capital sooner than that. As we shift to a virtual economy, jobs are diminishing. The nature of digital companies is that they employ fewer people and create more profits and grab more market share of companies from the past. That is only exacerbating that divide between capital and labour.

I think a digital dividend tax, a tax on companies that are harvesting our data for free, could help us to bridge this divide. Already states like California are considering this kind of a tax, in which companies that are getting the raw material, our data, for free, would have to put some of that wealth that they're extracting from surveillance capitalism back into public coffers. That could then be used for things like education, training a twenty-first-century labour market, helping to put broadband into rural areas and bring more people into the digital economy. Covid-19 has taught us that all things virtual are where the future is. If we can't operate in a digital economy, we may not be able to operate in any economy, but we need to make sure that the companies that are benefiting from these shifts are paying their fair share. A digital dividend tax could help rebalance power, not just between corporations and states, but between capital and labour, between companies and individuals.

ANTHONY TOWNSEND

RETHINKING ROBOTS

Science fiction is never just about the future. It is always just as much about the present: about our anxieties today, which we project into a (often dystopian) world to come. A hardy perennial of science fiction is the idea that robots take our jobs. Except that, as ever, science fiction has a habit of becoming everyday reality. Automation has caused unemployment. An increase in convenience for some consumers is a loss of jobs for other workers.

Convenience is the operative word there. Most product markets tend towards convenience in the end; the most successful and lucrative products in human history, like the smartphone, are the most convenient. But what exactly are we sacrificing on the altar of convenience? Our high streets are one thing; perhaps our planet is another. How might we harness the power of automation and robots to gain victories for the common good, rather than merely the satisfaction of immediate desires? As you'll read, in an exhilarating Asian experiment Townsend mentions, an early, incomplete answer to this question is already with us. It turns out the future is coming sooner than you thought.

For years, Americans had been surprisingly reluctant to shop for groceries online. As late as 2019, only about 4 per cent of us bought our food on a screen.

That is, until Covid-19 arrived in the spring of 2020, shuttering bricks and mortar retailers. Suddenly, twice as many grocery shoppers took to the web. This e-commerce surge quickly spread to other sectors as people prepared for a long lockdown. Amazon, for instance, saw a 20 per cent rise across the board in deliveries. For the first time ever, the company was forced to delay millions of deliveries – prioritising shipments of essential goods into the worst-afflicted cities.

In the end, the giant e-tailer's web of convenience held together. And as much as Americans had fearless frontline workers to thank, they also owed thanks to a horde of robots.

That's because – unlike meat-packing plants, the other piece of America's suddenly vulnerable supply chain – inside Amazon's massive, heavily automated 'fulfilment centres' an army of 100,000 self-driving sleds was doing much of the grunt work. Rocketing down aisles too narrow for humans to pass, at three times walking speed, they sped up the flow of goods *and* dramatically cut down on the amount of slow-motion human mingling on the warehouse floor. That helped keep Covid outbreaks at bay inside what was arguably the world's most important economic engine.

Many of the shops that closed that spring never reopened. Many were already on life support, after a decade of sluggish sales. E-commerce had been hollowing out high streets and malls for years. But Americans' stay-at-home shopping spree compressed years of economic change into a few short months.

I was torn. I mourned the city that's been lost, but I also wondered how we would retool our cities for an age where shutdowns may come without warning, and without end? Were the insides of these robo-warehouses a glimpse of our urban future?

Meanwhile, on the opposite side of the world, in Singapore, a new neighbourhood was taking shape. At Jurong Lake District, a second downtown was being built to absorb the island-nation's future growth. Planners were betting that a generation from now, two-thirds of our retail purchases will take place online rather than in person. What they were drafting was nothing less than a city without shops.

It was exciting to think of what we could do with all the recovered space. Grocery stores replaced with schools and concert halls, pharmacies giving way to wellness centres and spas ... assuming, of course, that in the future we would have conquered Covid-19 and could safely gather again.

As mind-blowing as it is though, I started to wonder … how will we move all that stuff? In cities today, kerbs are already blocked with delivery vans and building lobbies are overflowing with packages. What happens when we multiply the volume of stuff by a factor of five, ten or twenty?

The answer is quite straightforward. You simply build the city on top of a fulfilment centre.

Jurong Lake's plans detail a vast underground network of freight tunnels that will speed the flow of goods to homes and offices. Forget about same-day. Same-hour and even faster could become the norm when the warehouse is right under your feet. The cost and carbon footprint of delivery will collapse. Returns will be a breeze. And soon, sending stuff to anyone will cost about as much and be as easy as sending a text message.

This future felt far off. But during the summer of 2020, as I pondered the inevitable roar of Covid's second autumn wave, which would send us scurrying back to our homes, some version of Singapore's dream felt potentially close at hand. Would Americans find themselves peering hopefully out the window for the daily delivery, only to find one of those warehouse robots making a tentative test run down our street, goodies in tow? Empty streets and sidewalks would have to do, to take the place of cargo tunnels.

And even as vaccines promised to banish Covid-19 into the history books, it seemed inevitable that delivery droids were coming our way. We'd become hooked on shopping from home. The next great fortune, and the transportation revolution that will reshape our cities and towns, will go to those who figure out how to bring the things we need fastest to our front door.

Amol Rajan

POSTSCRIPT

Ensconced at the far end of the fourth floor of Old Broadcasting House, the historic home of the BBC, there sits an institution within an institution which, were it the possession of another country or culture, would prompt unbearable jealousy among our intelligentsia. Usefully, however, it is in fact British; and this jewel, replete with big ideas and outsized influence, is rightly the envy of the world.

Radio 4 is the sweet spot in the intersection of the Venn diagrams of intellectual ambition and public impact, both in Britain and, increasingly, the world. This accolade ought to belong to academia. For various historic reasons, it resides instead with the network that replaced the BBC Home Service in 1967. Academia can be too detached from the daily concerns of the public; and to some degree that can be its strength. Radio 4, however, derives value from delivering very clever stuff that a lot of the public want.

Rethink is supposed to the best of Radio 4, and therefore of the BBC. I'll let you be the judge of that. It is, in the best sense of that term, a brainchild; and it had two loving parents. First, Mohit Bakaya, the controller of Radio 4, who early in his reign was blessed with the intellectual challenge, and practical nightmare, of a once-in-a-century event. And second, Richard Knight, the genius commissioner for Radio 4, responsible for many of the best ideas currently on air in Britain. With their close involvement, the supremely erudite Peter Hanington of Radio 4 then masterminded the development of the project. All three have put me in a debt that may never be fully serviced.

Mohit's zealous ambition and leadership has been very keenly felt, not least when he rang me up and said he wanted the network to be home to the cleverest conversations about the pandemic anywhere in the world. To lean into not just how it will change the world, but how it should. Again, you can be the judge of whether we've pulled that off. For my part, I was so flattered by his call I immediately forgave his use of the phrase 'lean into', and said 'yes, please'. Like others involved in this project, I am grateful to Mohit for his kindness and gracious but firm insistence on the highest standards.

Rich and Pete are two other remarkable, and remarkably generous, Radio 4 brainiacs who wear their immense learning and wisdom lightly (Peter Hanington knocks out political thrillers – *A Single Source*, *A Dying Breed* – for fun). Their editorial judgement and creativity drove the commissioning process, and they, with Mohit, shepherded the essays collected in this book through the strands and sequence programmes on the network. If you consider *Rethink* anything other than a waste of time, this noble triarchy deserves your gratitude.

One of the things I have tried to do at the BBC is make more licence fee payers aware of the role of producers. I consumed countless hours of television in particular when I was growing up. But before I worked at the BBC, I didn't really know that most people who work there are producers.

Producers are the people who – like sub-editors in newspapers – deserve the most credit but generally get the least. Their job – logistical, editorial, financial, managerial – is to make programmes; presenters swan in later in the day and take all the glory, and most of the pay. Please permit me to name a few here.

Hugh Levinson, reliably dressed in floral print shirts, with dark wavy hair and trendy glasses, resembles a Reithian wizard, universally adored and respected, and has a legitimate claim to being the nicest and cleverest person I've met at the BBC.

My heartfelt thanks to several other outstanding colleagues: Ben Crighton, Ben Carter, Bob Howard, Alex Mansfield, Jim Frank, Smita Patel, Rosamund Jones, Louise Hidalgo, Derrick Bennett, Imogen Walford, Janet Staples, Lynda Davies and Bethan Jinkinson. They are the real heroes here. And so too of course are the superb studio engineers without whom this project would be silent: James Beard and Gareth Jones.

The team at BBC Books have been wonderful. Albert DePetrillo, Daniel Sørensen, Grace Paul, Abby Watson and Alice King all deserve huge thanks. But I'm especially grateful to Steve Tribe, whose editing has been superb and highly effective, and whose patience and judgement have made such a critical difference to these pages.

For the past few years, as I have reported on the most powerful companies in history, a nagging, gnawing sense that the great promise of technology was being betrayed, and that the very idea of a public domain was being reinvented but not very well, has grown. Several of the *Rethink* contributors make this point and, as one of life's optimists, I find it hard to admit that I do not think we are negotiating a very good deal with technology on behalf of civilisation.

The data kings of California have created addiction machines in which lies go viral faster than the truth; conspiracies are mainstreamed; disgusting abuse is an ineradicable constant; and civility and kindness are in short supply. Our shared space – our culture – has been poisoned, and with it the idea of the public as something ennobling has shrunk. David Marquand's *Decline of the Public* – published in March 2004, a month after Facebook was launched – is due a dark sequel.

If there is hope – and there is – I find it in Radio 4. And if there is hope, I see it in the people there. That is why I mention some above. Of course, there are many others.

Too busy playing cricket and dreaming of glory, I didn't grow up listening to the radio. In recent years, I have fallen in love with the medium. It derives an intimacy from being poured into our ears, because it feels like it belongs to us in that moment. And it is the kindest medium. Kind, because it doesn't reveal the receding hairlines or wrinkles of presenters; and kind because you can do other things, like drive or cook, while absorbing it.

Radio 4 – fountainhead to *Rethink* – is an amazing, precious property. What is more, if you're reading this in Britain, it is ours. I don't mean to make a parochial case here for the licence fee, or to rescue the BBC from its critics. I mean simply that if you believe the enervating tendencies of public life today are best met with the elevating power of ideas and culture, Radio 4 is busily at it on your behalf, all day, every day. I humbly commend it to all who have ears to lend, minds to open and cultures to enhance.

CONTRIBUTORS

REBECCA ADLINGTON

Rebecca Adlington is Great Britain's most successful ever swimmer. A four-time Olympic medallist in the 400m and 800m Freestyle, she won two Gold medals in Beijing 2008 and two Bronze medals in London 2012. Following her success in Beijing, she was awarded an OBE from the Queen at Buckingham Palace and accepted the Laureus World Sports Awards 'Breakthrough of the Year Award' from Sebastian Coe. She announced her retirement from elite swimming in 2013 and has since undertaken numerous roles in swimming commentary and punditry.

DOUGLAS ALEXANDER

The Rt. Hon. Douglas Alexander is a Senior Fellow at Harvard Kennedy School; Visiting Professor, King's College London; Trustee of the Royal United Services Institute; member of the European Council on Foreign Relations; and a Governor of the Ditchley Foundation. He was a Member of the UK Parliament 1997–2015, including serving in Cabinet as Secretary of State for International Development, UK's Governor to the World Bank, Secretary of State for Transport, Secretary of State for Scotland and Minister for Europe.

KWAME ANTHONY APPIAH

Kwame Anthony Appiah is Professor of Philosophy and Law at NYU. Earlier, he taught at Princeton, Harvard, Duke, Cornell, Yale, Cambridge and the University of Ghana. He grew up in Ghana and was educated at Cambridge, where he took BA and PhD degrees in philosophy. He has written widely in philosophy of mind and language, ethics and political philosophy. His most recent book is *The Lies that Bind: Rethinking Identity*.

AARON BASTANI

Aaron Bastani is a co-founder of Novara Media, a UK-based media outlet whose mission is to cover and examine the major challenges of the twenty-first century. He is also the author of *Fully Automated Luxury Communism: A Manifesto*, published by Verso Books in 2019. His next book, *Mortals*, will look at the political and economic implications of demographic ageing.

JUDE BROWNE

Professor Jude Browne is the Frankopan Director of the University of Cambridge Centre for Gender Studies, a Fellow of King's College and the Head of the Department of Politics and International Studies, University of

Cambridge (2021–2024). Her research interests are situated at the intersection of political theory and public policy and include gender inequality, the concept of the public interest and the impact of new technologies on society. Her current book project is on the topic of Political Responsibility.

CLARE CHAMBERS

Clare Chambers is Professor of Political Philosophy and a Fellow of Jesus College at the University of Cambridge. She is the author of *Against Marriage: An Egalitarian Defence of the Marriage-Free State* (Oxford University Press, 2017), *Sex, Culture, and Justice: The Limits of Choice* (Penn State University Press, 2008) and *Teach Yourself Political Philosophy: A Complete Introduction* with Phil Parvin (Hodder, 2012). Her next book, a defence of the unmodified body, will be published by Allen Lane.

JARVIS COCKER

Jarvis Cocker formed the much-loved Pulp aged 15 and has subsequently made solo records, hosted his own hugely popular radio show, and had a selection of his lyrics published by Faber & Faber in his book *Mother, Brother, Lover*. His new work, *This Book Is a Song*, will be published by Jonathan Cape.

CAROL COOPER

Carol Cooper is an award-winning consultant specialising in equitable leadership and racial trauma. She began a career in nursing over 30 years ago but her origins as a Jamaican woman born in the UK meant that she continued to observe and experience a systemic exclusion which threatened to limit, erase and silence people who looked like her. Curiosity, love and a refusal to accept inequality as standard, gave her the courage, which would carve out the insight she now uses to advise leaders across the globe about matters pertaining to racial equity. Working across the public and private sector, she creates opportunities to disrupt, reimagine, redefine and construct an equitable ecosystem, where all races are equally valued.

THE DALAI LAMA

His Holiness the Dalai Lama is the spiritual leader of Tibetan Buddhists and a Nobel laureate.

JARED DIAMOND

Jared Diamond is a Pulitzer-prize-winning author of five best-selling books, translated into 38 languages, about human societies and human evolution: *Guns, Germs and Steel, Collapse, Why Is Sex Fun?, The Third Chimpanzee* and *The World until Yesterday*. As a professor of geography at UCLA (University of California at Los Angeles), he is known for his breadth of interests, which involves conducting research and teaching in three other fields: the biology of New Guinea birds, digestive physiology and conservation biology. His prizes and honours include the US National

Medal of Science, the Pulitzer Prize for Non-fiction, the Tyler Prize for Environmental Science and election to the US National Academy of Sciences. He is a director of World Wildlife Fund/US and of Conservation International. As a biological explorer, his most widely publicised finding was his rediscovery, at the top of New Guinea's remote Foja Mountains, of the long-lost Golden-fronted Bowerbird, previously known only from four specimens found in a Paris feather shop in 1895.

HENRY DIMBLEBY

Henry Dimbleby has been a lead non-executive board member of the Department for Environment, Food and Rural Affairs since March 2018. In June 2019 he was appointed to lead the National Food Strategy. He co-founded Leon restaurants chain, was a co-founder of the Sustainable Restaurant Association and co-authored *The School Food Plan* (2013). He previously worked as a commis chef at the Michelin-starred Inn on the Park, as a journalist, and as a Strategy Consultant at Bain & Company (1995–2002).

SEB EMINA

Seb Emina is editor in chief of *The Happy Reader*, the literary magazine published by Penguin in collaboration with *Fantastic Man*. His writing has appeared in publications including the *New York Times*, *Paris Review*, *FT Weekend*, *Guardian Review*, *Gentlewoman*, *Telegraph Travel* and *Vogue*.

He is the co-author of *The Breakfast Bible* (2013) and the co-creator of globalbreakfastradio.com, a perpetual morning-radio aggregator. He lives between Paris and London.

BRIAN ENO

Musician, producer, visual artist and activist Brian Eno first came to international prominence in the early 1970s as a founding member of British band Roxy Music, followed by a series of solo albums and collaborations. His work as producer includes albums with Talking Heads, Devo, U2, Laurie Anderson and Coldplay, while his list of collaborations include recordings with David Bowie, Jon Hassell, David Byrne, Grace Jones, James Blake and most recently with brother Roger on *Mixing Colours*. His visual experiments with light and video continue to parallel his musical career, with exhibitions and installations all over the globe. He is a founding member of the Long Now Foundation, a trustee of Client Earth and patron of Videre est Credere. His latest album, *Film Music 1976–2020*, was released in November 2020.

CALEB FEMI

Caleb Femi is a multi-disciplined creative who uses film, photography and music to push the boundaries of poetry both on the page, in performance and on digital mediums. He has written and directed short films commissioned by the BBC and Channel 4 and poems by the Tate Modern, the Royal Society for Literature, St Paul's Cathedral, the BBC, *The Guardian* and many more. Once the Young People's Laureate for London, he recently released a critically acclaimed poetry collection, *Poor*.

NIALL FERGUSON

Niall Ferguson, MA, D.Phil., FRSE, is the Milbank Family Senior Fellow at the Hoover Institution, Stanford University, and a senior faculty fellow of the Belfer Center for Science and International Affairs at Harvard. He is also a visiting professor at Tsinghua University, Beijing. He is the author of sixteen books, including *The Pity of War*, *The House of Rothschild*, *Empire: How Britain Made the Modern World*, *Civilization* and *Kissinger, 1923–1968: The Idealist*.

RANA FOROOHAR

Rana Foroohar is Global Business Columnist and an Associate Editor at the *Financial Times*, based in New York. She is also CNN's global economic analyst. Her first book, *Makers and Takers: The Rise of Finance and the Fall of American Business* was shortlisted for the FT and McKinsey Book of the Year award in 2016. Her second book, *Don't Be Evil: How Big Tech Betrayed Its Founding Principles – And All of Us*, about the 20-year rise of platform technology and how it has reshaped economics, politics and society, was released in November of 2019. She is a member of the Council on Foreign Relations, and sits on the advisory board of the Open Markets Institute.

PETER FRANKOPAN

Peter Frankopan is Professor of Global History at Oxford University. His books include *The Silk Roads: A New History of the World*, a global bestseller that has been translated into 35 languages and *The New Silk Roads: The Present and Future of the World*, which was awarded the Carical Prize in 2019, when he also won Germany's Calliope Prize. He advises governments, multilateral organisations and corporations about the world of the past, present and future.

NICCI GERRARD

Nicci Gerrard is a journalist, a novelist (writing under her own name and as half of the psychological thriller writer Nicci French) and the co-founder of John's Campaign, which fights for the rights of people living with dementia and those who care for them. In 2016 she won the Orwell Prize for her campaigning journalism; her book, *What Dementia Teaches Us About Love*, published in 2019, sets out to change the way we think about age and vulnerability.

ANAND GIRIDHARADAS

Anand Giridharadas is the author of *Winners Take All: The Elite Charade of Changing the World*, published by Knopf in 2018. His other books are *The True American: Murder and Mercy in Texas*, about a Muslim immigrant's campaign to spare from Death Row the white supremacist who tried to kill him; and *India Calling: An Intimate Portrait of a Nation's Remaking*, about returning to the India his parents left. He is an editor-at-large for *TIME*, an on-air political analyst for MSNBC and a visiting scholar at the Arthur L. Carter Journalism Institute at New York University. He is a former columnist and correspondent for the *New York Times*, and has also written for *The Times*, *The Atlantic*, *The New Yorker* and elsewhere.

DAVID GRAEBER

David Graeber (1961–2020) was an American anthropologist, activist and author known for his books *Debt: The First 5000 Years*, *The Utopia of Rules*, *Bullshit Jobs: A Theory* and the forthcoming *The Dawn of Everything: A New History of Humanity* (2021). He was a professor of anthropology at the London School of Economics.

KATHERINE GRAINGER

Dame Katherine Grainger is the current Chair of UK Sport. She is Britain's most decorated female Olympic athlete and the first British woman to win medals at five successive Olympic Games. A Fellow of King's College and a Regent of Edinburgh University, she is currently Chancellor of Glasgow University. For services to rowing, she was awarded an MBE in 2006 and a CBE in 2013. She serves as an ambassador, patron or board member of various charities and sporting bodies and this was recognised when she became Dame Katherine Grainger in the 2017 New Year's Honours List for services to sport and charity.

EMMA GRIFFIN

Emma Griffin is Professor of British History at UEA. She is the author of five books, including most recently *Bread Winner: An Intimate History of the Victorian Economy* and is currently writing a global history of industrialisation. She is the President of the Royal Historical Society and a co-editor of the *Historical Journal*.

MOHAMMED HANIF

Mohammed Hanif was born in Okara, Pakistan. He graduated from the Pakistan Air Force Academy as Pilot Officer but subsequently left to pursue a career in journalism. He has written for stage, film and BBC Radio. His first novel, *A Case of Exploding Mangoes*, was longlisted for the Man Booker Prize, shortlisted for The Guardian First Book Award and won the Commonwealth Writers' Prize for Best First Novel. He was the head of the BBC Urdu Service in London and now works as their special correspondent based in Karachi.

JAMES HARDING

James Harding is the co-founder and Editor of Tortoise Media, and prior to this was Director of News and Current Affairs at the BBC, the world's largest news organisation. He was the Editor of *The Times* from 2007 to 2012, winning the Newspaper of the Year in two of the five years he edited the paper. He was previously *The Times*'s Business Editor, having joined from the *Financial Times*, where he worked as Washington Bureau Chief, Media Editor and China correspondent opening the paper's bureau in Shanghai in 1996. He is the author of *Alpha Dogs: How Political Spin Became a Global Business*, and he presented *On Background* on the BBC World Service with Zanny Minton-Beddoes, Editor of *The Economist*.

PETER HENNESSY

Lord Hennessy is Attlee Professor of Contemporary British History at Queen Mary University of London and a Fellow of the British Academy. He was created an independent crossbench peer in 2010 and sits on the House of Lords Constitution Committee. His books include a 'post-war trilogy' (*Never Again: Britain 1945–51*, *Having It So Good: Britain in the Fifties* and *Winds of Change: Britain in the Early Sixties*). He has also written *Cabinet*, *Whitehall* and *The Prime Minister*.

BRENDA HALE

The Rt. Hon. the Baroness Hale of Richmond retired as President of the Supreme Court of the United Kingdom in January 2020, after 26 years as a full-time judge in the High Court, Court of Appeal, House of Lords and Supreme Court. Before that, she was an academic at the University of Manchester for 18 years and then a Law Commissioner for nine, specializing in family, welfare and equality law.

REED HASTINGS

Reed Hastings co-founded Netflix in 1997. He is an active educational philanthropist and served on the California State Board of Education from 2000 to 2004. He is currently on the board of several educational organisations including KIPP, Pahara and The City Fund. He has a BA from Bowdoin College and an MSCS in Artificial Intelligence from Stanford University. Between studying, he served in the Peace Corps as a high school math teacher in Swaziland.

COLIN JACKSON

Colin Jackson CBE is a multi-medal former sprinter and hurdling athlete. He has been an integral part of BBC programming for all major athletic events, including the Olympic Games in London in 2012 and in Rio de Janeiro in 2016. He works closely with Sport Relief, where he is a member of the steering panel, and is also an International Inspiration Ambassador for UNICEF as well as founding and fronting the Go Dad Run campaign for Prostate Cancer.

LUCY JONES

Lucy Jones is the author of *Losing Eden: Why Our Minds Need The Wild* and *Foxes Unearthed*, winner of the Society of Authors' Roger Deakin Award. Her journalism on culture, science and nature has been published in BBC Earth, BBC Wildlife, the *Sunday Times*, *The Guardian* and the *New Statesman*. She is based in Hampshire, England.

KANG KYUNG-WHA

Kang Kyung-wha is a South Korean diplomat and politician who served as the first Foreign Minister of South Korea under President Moon Jae-in from 2017 to 2021 and was the first woman to hold the position. She previously worked for the Korean Broadcasting System as a producer of English Service Division of Radio Korea. She lectured at Cleveland State University, Ohio and Sejong University, Seoul as an associate professor. She was also the spokeswoman of the Korean Women's NGO Committee for the Beijing Conference in 1995, a member of International Relations Committee of Korean National Council of Women and a director of Korean Institute for Women and Politics.

NISHA KATONA

Nisha Katona MBE is a British-born Indian, dedicated curry evangelist and founder of Mowgli Street Food. Author of *Pimp My Rice*, *The Spice Tree* and *Mowgli Street Food*, she regularly appears on television and radio as a restaurant, food and business expert. Prior to taking on the restaurant business, she worked as a full-time barrister for 20 years before giving up the security of the Bar to dedicate herself to her restaurants, her food writing and her curry evangelism.

PAUL KRUGMAN

Paul Krugman is best known to the general public as Opinion Columnist for the *New York Times*, a position he has held since 2000. In his academic life, he is Distinguished Professor in Economics at the City University of New York (CUNY) Graduate Center, a core faculty member at the Stone Center on Socio-Economic Inequality, and Luxembourg Income Study (LIS) Senior Scholar. He was the sole recipient of the Nobel Prize in Economic Sciences in 2008 for his work on international trade theory and the geographic distribution of economic activity.

C.K. LAL

C.K. Lal is a columnist for the *Kathmandu Post* (English) and the *Kantipur Dainik* (Nepali) newspapers. He has been writing regularly for various publications of South Asia for over three decades. In 2006, he was voted the most influential columnist of Nepal. He was an Asia Leadership Fellow in 2008 in Japan and a Poynter Fellow at Yale University in 2013. His published books include *Nepaliya Hunlai* (Nepali), *To be Nepalese* (English) and *Mithila Manthan* (Maithili) and *Human Rights, Governance and Democracy* (English).

AMANDA LEVETE

Amanda Levete is a Stirling Prize winning architect and founder of AL_A, an award-winning architectural practice. Recently completed projects include the Victoria & Albert Museum Exhibition Road Quarter (2017) in London and MAAT (2016), a Museum of Art, Architecture and Technology in Lisbon. She is a regular radio and TV broadcaster and lectures throughout the world. In 2017, she was recognised in the Queen's Birthday Honours list and made a CBE for services to architecture.

Margaret MacMillan

Margaret MacMillan is a Canadian historian who works mainly on the twentieth century. She was Warden of St Antony's College, Oxford, in 2007–2017, and she is a Fellow of the Royal Society of Literature, an Honorary Fellow of St Antony's College, Oxford and an Honorary Fellow of the British Academy. She is an expert on history and international relations, and was the 2018 Reith lecturer, giving five lectures across the globe on the theme of war. Her latest book is *War: How Conflict Shaped Us*.

Carolyn McCall

Carolyn became ITV's Chief Executive in January 2018 and launched a review of the company's strategy in light of the rapidly changing media landscape. Before this she was Chief Executive of easyJet for over seven years, where she led a turnaround, and had previously held various commercial and management roles at the Guardian Media Group, including CEO of the *Guardian* and *Observer* before becoming Group CEO in 2006. In 2016 Carolyn was awarded a Damehood for services to the aviation industry having received an OBE in 2008 for services to women in business.

GINA MCCARTHY

Gina McCarthy is National Climate Advisor to US President Joseph Biden. She was previously the president and chief executive officer of NRDC (Natural Resources Defense Council), served as US Environmental Protection Agency administrator under President Obama, and has advised six governors. She was also a professor at Harvard University's T.H. Chan School of Public Health, and chair of the board of advisors at the Harvard Center for Climate, Health and the Global Environment (C-CHANGE).

H.R. MCMASTER

H.R. McMaster is a Senior Fellow at the Hoover Institution, a Fellow at the Freeman Spogli Institute and Lecturer at the Graduate School of Business at Stanford University. He retired from the US Army in 2018 as Lieutenant General, served as the 26th National Security Adviser and is the award-winning author of *Battlegrounds* and *Dereliction of Duty*.

ELIZA MANNINGHAM BULLER

The Rt. Hon. the Baroness Manningham Buller has been Chair of Wellcome since 2015, having served as a Governor since 2008. She was appointed to the House of Lords in 2008 and sits as an independent, crossbench peer. She has been a member of the Joint Committee on the National Security Strategy and is currently serving her second term on the Science and Technology select committee. Her 33 years in MI5, the UK's security service, culminated in her appointment as Director General in 2002. She was a Reith Lecturer in 2011 and made a Lady Companion of the Order of the Garter in 2014.

MARIANA MAZZUCATO

Mariana Mazzucato is Professor in the Economics of Innovation and Public Value at University College London (UCL) where she is Founding Director of the Institute for Innovation and Public Purpose (IIPP). She advises policymakers around the world on innovation-led inclusive and sustainable growth. She is author of *The Entrepreneurial State: Debunking Public vs. Private Sector Myths* (2013), *The Value of Everything: Making and Taking in the Global Economy* (2018) and *Mission Economy: A Moonshot Guide to Changing Capitalism* (2020). She is winner of international prizes including the 2020 John Von Neumann Award and the 2019 All European Academies Madame de Staël Prize for Cultural Values.

MIRABELLE MORAH

Mirabelle Morah experiments on growth-hacking strategies to see how storytelling, tech and digital media can be used for societal good, especially with social enterprises or people-powered campaigns. She is the 22-year-old founder of BlankPaperz Media, a platform that amplifies the projects and voices of young Africans finding solutions to problems that affect their societies. She is also the Editorial and Communications Head of Z'axis e-Magazine, a founding member of Chatham House's (the Royal Institute of International Affairs) Common Futures Conversations Platform, and is one of We Are Family Foundation's Young Global Leaders.

ONORA O'NEILL

Onora O'Neill combines writing on political philosophy and ethics with public life. She has been a crossbench member of the House of Lords since 2000, and is an Emeritus Honorary Professor of Philosophy at Cambridge. She writes on justice and ethics, accountability and trust, and the ethics of communication.

STEVEN PINKER

Steven Pinker is a Johnstone Family Professor in the Department of Psychology at Harvard University. He conducts research on language and cognition, writes for publications such as the *New York Times*, *Time* and *The Atlantic*, and is the author of ten books, including *The Language Instinct*, *How the Mind Works*, *The Blank Slate*, *The Stuff of Thought*, *The Better Angels of Our Nature*, *The Sense of Style*, and most recently, *Enlightenment Now: The Case for Reason, Science, Humanism, and Progress*.

POPE FRANCIS

Francis (Jorge Mario Bergoglio), the 266th Bishop of Rome, is the first Jesuit pope, and the first from Latin America.

After 13 years as cardinal archbishop of Buenos Aires, he was elected in March 2013, taking the name Francis. In December 2020, he published a reflection on the Covid crisis, *Let Us Dream: The Path to a Better Future*.

SAMANTHA POWER

Ambassador Samantha Power is Professor of Practice at Harvard Kennedy School and Harvard Law School. From 2013 to 2017, she served as the United States Ambassador to the United Nations and as a member of President Barack Obama's cabinet. She is the author of books including *'A Problem from Hell': America and the Age of Genocide*, which won the Pulitzer Prize in 2003, and the recent memoir *The Education of an Idealist*.

AMOL RAJAN

Amol Rajan is a broadcaster for the BBC. A presenter on Radio 4's flagship *Today* programme and BBC One's prime-time magazine programme *The One Show*, he is also Media Editor for BBC News, leading the Corporation's coverage of media and technology globally. On Radio 4 he is a presenter of *Start the Week* and *Rethink*, and he presents current affairs documentaries for BBC Two. Appointed Editor of *The Independent* aged 29, he was for several years a restaurant critic, leading to occasional appearances on *Masterchef*. He spent his gap year at the Foreign and Commonwealth Office, before reading English at Downing College, University of

Cambridge. His first book, *Twirlymen*, was a history of spin bowling. He is the co-founder of KEY Sessions, a charity for inner-city teenagers in London.

V.S. RAMACHANDRAN

V.S. Ramachandran is Director of the Center for Brain and Cognition, Distinguished Professor with the Psychology Department and Neurosciences Program at the University of California, San Diego, and Adjunct Professor of Biology at the Salk Institute. He initially trained as a doctor at Stanley Medical College, Madras, India. His early work was on visual perception but he is best known for his experiments in behavioural neurology which, despite their apparent simplicity, have had a profound impact on the way we think about the brain. He has been called 'the Marco Polo of neuroscience' by Richard Dawkins.

CHARLOTTE LYDIA RILEY

Dr Charlotte Lydia Riley is Lecturer in twentieth-century British history at the University of Southampton. She writes and teaches about British identity, politics and society, including the history of the Labour Party and the history of the British feminist movement. She is writing a book, *Imperial Island*, which explores how British society, politics and culture have been shaped by empire and decolonisation.

TOM RIVETT-CARNAC

Tom Rivett-Carnac is an author, podcaster and political strategist who has worked for 20 years on solutions to the climate crisis. He is co-author of *The Future We Choose: The Stubborn Optimists' Guide to the Climate Crisis* and co-host of the podcast *Outrage and Optimism*. From 2013 to 2016 he was the senior political strategist at the UN Climate Convention and as such is regarded as one of the architects of the historic Paris Agreement on Climate Change. In 2016 he co-founded Global Optimism with Christiana Figueres, based on the conviction that the years to 2030 will determine humanity's future. From that platform he continues to work on transformative change for a regenerative world at the highest levels of business and government.

CARLO ROVELLI

Carlo Rovelli is a theoretical physicist, known for his work in the field of quantum gravity and on the conceptual foundations of physics. He was born in Italy in 1956 and has worked in universities in Italy, the United States and France. He has written several popular science bestsellers, including *Seven Brief Lessons in Physics* (on modern physics), *The Order of Time* (on the nature of time) and *Helgoland* (on quantum theory).

STUART RUSSELL

Stuart Russell is Professor of Computer Science at Berkeley, an Honorary Fellow of Wadham College, Oxford, and an Andrew Carnegie Fellow. He is a leading researcher in artificial intelligence and the author (with Peter Norvig) of *Artificial Intelligence: A Modern Approach*, the standard text in the field. He has been active in arms control for nuclear and autonomous weapons. His latest book, *Human Compatible*, addresses the long-term impact of AI on humanity.

ZIAUDDIN SARDAR

Ziauddin Sardar, award-winning writer and cultural critic, is former Professor of Law and Society at Middlesex University, and editor of the quarterly *Critical Muslim*. Considered a pioneering writer on Islam and contemporary cultural issues, he has published over fifty books, including his acclaimed autobiography, *Desperately Seeking Paradise: Journeys of a Sceptical Muslim* and, more recently, *Mecca: The Sacred City* and *The Postnormal Times Reader*.

ELIF SHAFAK

Elif Shafak is an award-winning British-Turkish novelist. Her latest novel, *10 Minutes 38 Seconds in this Strange World*, was shortlisted for the Booker Prize and RSL Ondaatje Prize. Her previous novel, *The Forty Rules of Love*, was chosen by BBC among 100 Novels that Shaped Our World. She holds a PhD in political science and has taught at various universities in Turkey, the USA and the UK, including St Anne's College, Oxford University, where she is an honorary fellow. She is a Fellow and a Vice President of the Royal Society of Literature. She is a member of Weforum Global Agenda Council on Creative Economy and a founding member of ECFR (European Council on Foreign Relations). In 2017 she was chosen by Politico as one of the twelve people 'who will give you a much needed lift of the heart'.

K.K. SHAILAJA

Popularly known as Shailaja Teacher, K.K. Shailaja is an Indian politician and Minister of Health and Social Welfare for Kerala state.

AMONGE SINXOTO

Amonge Sinxoto is a 19-year-old youth activist, social entrepreneur, public speaker and 2019's Global Teen Leader. She is an authentically African creative with a burning desire to represent what she feels it means to be an African youth in the twenty-first century. As the founder of Blackboard Africa, a youth Non-Profit Company, she is at the forefront of driving the narrative of the continent into a new direction.

DAVID SKELTON

David Skelton is author of *Little Platoons: How a Revived One Nation can Empower England's Forgotten Towns and Redraw the Political Map*. He has written widely about the need to revive 'left behind' towns, reform the economy so that it works in the interests of all citizens and create a fairer deal for the low paid. Previously, he founded Renewal with the goal of broadening the appeal of the Tory Party and was Head of Research at Policy Exchange.

GEORGE SOROS

George Soros is founder and chair of Soros Fund Management and the Open Society Foundations. Born in Budapest, he survived the Nazi occupation and fled Hungary in 1947 for England and graduated from the London School of Economics. He then settled in the USA and accumulated a large fortune through the investment fund he founded. Active as a philanthropist since 1979, he has given away more than $32 billion. The Open Society Foundations support individuals and organisations in over 120 countries, working to build inclusive democracies. He has authored over a dozen books, including *In Defense of Open Society* (2019).

EVAN SPIEGEL

Evan Spiegel, who graduated from Stanford University with a BS in Product Design, is Co-Founder and Chief Executive Officer at the camera company Snap Inc. The company believes that reinventing the camera represents their greatest opportunity to improve the way people live and communicate. Their products empower people to express themselves, live in the moment, learn about the world and have fun together.

JONATHAN SUMPTION

The Rt. Hon. Lord Sumption began his career as a Fellow in History of Magdalen College, Oxford, before changing career and becoming a barrister. He was appointed a Justice of the Supreme Court straight from the bar in 2012. After retiring from the Court in 2018, he delivered the BBC Reith Lectures for 2019 on 'Law and the Decline of Politics' (published by Profile Books as *Trials of the State*).

ANTHONY TOWNSEND

Dr Anthony Townsend works at the intersection of urbanisation and digital technology. He is Urbanist in Residence at Cornell Tech's Jacobs Institute, where his research focuses on scenarios and ethical frameworks for urban tech innovation. Anthony is the author of two books, *Ghost Road: Beyond the Driverless Car* (2020) and *Smart Cities: Big Data, Civic Hackers and the Quest for A New Utopia* (2013), both published by W.W. Norton & Co.

KT TUNSTALL

KT Tunstall is a singer-songwriter and musician who scored a worldwide smash in 2004 with her debut album, *Eye To The Telescope*, which went on to sell over 5 million copies. She has remained at the forefront of UK singer-songwriter talent. She followed up that early success with albums *Drastic Fantastic*, *Tiger Suit*, *Invisible Empire // Crescent Moon*, *KIN* and *WAX* in 2007, 2010, 2013, 2016 and 2018 respectively, cementing her reputation as a major recording talent, as well as a mesmerising live artist.

MATTHEW WALKER

Matthew Walker earned his PhD in neuroscience from the Medical Research Council in London, UK, and subsequently became Professor of Psychiatry at Harvard Medical School. He is currently Professor of Neuroscience and Psychology at the University of California, Berkeley, and director of the Center for Human Sleep Science. In 2017, he published the acclaimed international bestseller, *Why We Sleep: Unlocking the Power of Sleep and Dreams*, which provides a complete description of, and prescription for, sleep.

DAVID WALLACE-WELLS

David Wallace-Wells is a columnist and deputy editor at *New York* magazine. He has been a national fellow at the New America Foundation and was previously the deputy editor of the *Paris Review*. He writes frequently about climate change and the near future of science and technology. In July 2017 he published a cover story surveying the landscape of worst-case scenarios for global warming that became an immediate sensation, reaching millions of readers on its first day and, in less than a week, becoming the most-read story the magazine had ever published and sparking an unprecedented debate, ongoing still today among scientists and journalists, about just how we should be thinking, and talking, about the planetary threat from climate change.

TARA WESTOVER

Tara Westover is an American memoirist and historian. Her first book, *Educated* (2018), debuted at number 1 on the *New York Times* bestseller list, and was a finalist for a number of awards, including the National Book Critics Circle Award, the LA Times Book Prize and the PEN/Jean Stein Book Award. *Educated* remained on the New York Times list for more than two years in hardcover, and has been translated into 46 languages.

XINE YAO

Dr Xine Yao is Lecturer in American Literature to 1900 at University College London. Her first book is *Disaffected: The Cultural Politics of Unfeeling in Nineteenth-Century America* (Duke University Press, 2021). Her honours include the American Studies Association's Yasuo Sakakibara Essay Prize and her research has been supported by grants from the Social Sciences and Humanities Research Council of Canada. She is a BBC Radio 3 / AHRC New Generation Thinker and the co-host of PhDivas Podcast.

CREDITS

Rethinking Humanity © Carlo Rovelli
Rethinking Poverty © Pope Francis
Rethinking Democracy © Peter Hennessy
Rethinking Capitalism © Anand Giridharadas
Rethinking a Global Response © Jared Diamond
Rethinking Normality © Ziauddin Sardar
Rethinking Ancient Wisdom © Dalai Lama
Rethinking Institutions © C.K. Lal
Rethinking an Environmental Revolution © Jarvis Cocker
Rethinking the Body © Clare Chambers
Rethinking Human Nature © Steven Pinker
Rethinking History © Tom Rivett-Carnac
Rethinking the State © Jonathan Sumption
Rethinking Industry © David Skelton
Rethinking Work © Emma Griffin
Rethinking Education © Caleb Femi
Rethinking Activism © Gina McCarthy
Rethinking the Education Divide © Tara Westover
Rethinking the Power of Small Actions © Kwame Anthony
  Appiah
Rethinking Universities © Charlotte Riley
Rethinking Development © K.K. Shailaja
Rethinking Global Governance © Samantha Power
Rethinking the Music Industry © KT Tunstall
Rethinking the Athlete's Life © Rebecca Adlington
Rethinking How We Do Trials © Brenda Hale
Rethinking Hospitality © Nisha Katona
Rethinking the Olympics © Katherine Grainger
Rethinking Jobs © David Graeber
Rethinking News © James Harding
Rethinking Television © Carolyn McCall

343

Rethinking Intimacy © Mohammad Hanif
Rethinking Empathy © H.R. McMaster
Rethinking Racial Equality © Carol Cooper
Rethinking Solidarity © Paul Krugman
Rethinking Safety © Amonge Sinxoto
Rethinking Togetherness © Reed Hastings
Rethinking Accountability © Kang Kyung-wha
Rethinking Biophilia © Lucy Jones
Rethinking Our Responsibility for Our Health © Colin Jackson
Rethinking Ourselves © Mirabelle Morah
Rethinking Old Age © Nicci Gerrard
Rethinking the Winners © Brian Eno
Rethinking Responsibility © Jude Browne
Rethinking Uncertainty © Elif Shafak
Rethinking How We Live © Amanda Levete
Rethinking Progress © Niall Ferguson
Rethinking Consensus © David Wallace-Wells
Rethinking International Cooperation © Margaret MacMillan
Rethinking Nature © HRH The Prince of Wales
Rethinking Digital Power © Onora O'Neill
Rethinking Sleep © Matthew Walker
Rethinking How We Eat © Henry Dimbleby
Rethinking Health Inequality © Eliza Manningham-Buller
Rethinking Masks © Xine Yao
Rethinking Debt © George Soros
Rethinking Value © Mariana Mazzucato
Rethinking Economic Dignity © Douglas Alexander
Rethinking Long-Term Success © Evan Spiegel
Rethinking Asia © Peter Frankopan
Rethinking AI © Stuart Russell
Rethinking Brains © V.S. Ramachandran
Rethinking Travel © Seb Emina
Rethinking an Aging Population © Aaron Bastani
Rethinking Data © Rana Foroohar
Rethinking Robots © Anthony Townsend